The Green Socialist

Zack Polanski and the Battle for Britain's Future

Russell Warfield

PLUTO PRESS

First published 2026 by Pluto Press
New Wing, Somerset House, Strand, London WC2R 1LA
and Pluto Press, Inc.
1930 Village Center Circle, 3-834, Las Vegas, NV 89134
www.plutobooks.com

A CIP catalogue record for this book is available from the British Library

978-0-7453-5268-8 (paperback)
978-0-7453-5270-1 (.epub)
978-0-7453-5269-5 (.pdf)

Typesetting by Jamie Bowman
Cover design by Melanie Patrick
Cover image: Mark Thomas/Alamy Live News

Printed in the United Kingdom

EU GPSR Authorised Representative
LOGOS EUROPE, 9 rue Nicolas Poussin, 17000, LA ROCHELLE, France
Email: contact@logoseurope.eu

The Green Socialist

'Russell Warfield expertly traces how successive crises of global capitalism have exposed the divide between the 1% benefitting from our economic model, and the 99% suffering from it. Warfield shows that ecosocialism is the only answer to the crises we face. Essential reading for any serious left organiser.'

—Grace Blakeley, author of *Vulture Capitalism*

'A much-needed book. Brilliantly explains that the Green Party was in search of a leader like Polanski and why we should not be surprised that this is a movement still moving leftwards.'

—Danny Dorling, author of *The Next Crisis*

'A serious and much-needed book that challenges the media belief in the Zack Polanski surge as a flash in the pan, and argues for the viability of the Green Party in England and Wales as a necessary political vehicle for the transformation of the whole country.'

—James Meadway, host of *Macrodose* podcast

'Russell has been in the heart of the Greens for all our major steps forward over the past decade, so this action-packed must-read is for anyone wanting to understand how the party seems to have come out of nowhere to strike a chord with a new generation.'

—Sian Berry MP

'We know the British Left is in urgent need of a new politics. In *The Green Socialist*, Russell Warfield makes a nuanced, compelling case that Zack Polanski's leadership of the Green Party now offers our best chance of defeating the rising racist, reactionary politics of our time through his commitment to an egalitarian, eco-populism capable of reviving the Left in our warming world. Beautifully written, this book deserves a wide readership.'

—Lynne Segal, author of *Lean on Me: A Politics of Radical Care*

'Brilliantly written, *The Green Socialist* offers an unparalleled inside track on both Polanski the figure and the movement behind him, seamlessly shifting gears between deep history and fresh analysis. This is the outstanding read on the new Green left of the 2020s – insightful, entertaining and essential.'

—Michael Chessum, author of *This Is Just The Beginning: The Making of a New Left, From Anti-Austerity to the Fall of Corbyn*

'Polanski's success as the Greens' leader has stirred conversations about the party's formation, its politics and trajectory. Warfield's fantastic book answers those questions and then some, scoping the tensions, controversies and opportunities that await this insurgent eco-populism. It's an essential read.'

—Jonas Patrick Marvin, cohost of *Life of the Party* podcast and author of *The Breaking of the English Working Class*

'*The Green Socialist* is a brilliantly readable, insightful, balanced and optimistic account of arguably the most important political development of our times: the emergence of the Green Party as a serious electoral force to Labour's left.'

—Jeremy Gilbert, author of *Twenty-First Century Socialism*

For Eden, Primrose and Lumi

Contents

INTRODUCTION

The Return of the 99%

Everything is falling apart. For nearly half a century, the foundations of a good quality of life have been eroded by a political system which has privatised our shared assets, shrunk the public realm and trashed our planet. For a time, the ostensible compensation for this was cheap credit for consumers and a flood of readily available material goods. But the 2008 financial crisis hit that economic settlement like a meteorite, presenting problems for which nobody among the ruling class has yet found answers. Growth, living standards and wages have been sluggish or stagnant ever since.[1] Now a series of extreme shocks in the 2020s – from the social disaster of Covid to double-digit inflation – have turned that stagnation into a freefall decline from which few of us are completely insulated.

This economy based on unrestrained extraction, consumption and waste is what drives the destruction of our natural world. Seven out of nine identified planetary limits are now breached.[2]

Rather than change course following the 2008 crash, politicians across the West have stood around the decaying corpse of this economic model, deluding themselves into believing that it might yet be revived. Nothing they try works. Here in the UK, runways and roads are promised in the name of growth. Such magical thinking has no effect on the economy, but the environmental destruction continues. In 2026, a UK government national security assessment judged our ecological crisis to be a national security risk, presenting overlapping threats ranging from food shortages to infectious disease outbreaks.[3]

If you put on the news, you'd think there's absolutely nothing we can do about any of this. The managerial class of mainstream politicians – shuffling through prime ministers at an unprecedented speed in recent years – basically shrug, mumbling that they can only try to manage the decline as competently as possible. Some hoped that the first Labour administration in 14 years would at least alleviate the worst symptoms of our overlapping crises. What they got was a government which doubled down on punitive cruelty towards migrants, abandoned many of its climate commitments, further savaged the welfare state and embroiled itself in justifying genocide.

The result is a collapse in political legitimacy. Polling shows an unprecedented lack of belief in the ability of either of the two main parties to turn this situation around, or indeed even in the principle of democracy itself. The National Centre of Social Research observes that elections tend to repair and restore trust in the political process. No longer. Following the 2024 general election, trust in governments to put the nation's interest above party interest hit an all-time low of 12 per cent.[4] Meanwhile, this decade has seen, for the first time ever, more people supporting changes to the voting system than those wanting to keep it as it is – a gap that is now growing every year.[5]

The most notable potential escape from this trajectory came in the form of Jeremy Corbyn's Labour Party, which, in the general election of 2017, came within touching distance of winning state power on a programme that promised investment in the public sector and nationalisation of the main utilities. While Corbynism was obliterated in the general election of 2019, one of the legacies of this period of British politics has been to permanently widen political horizons and raise political hopes. In the immediate term, however, the main consequence of Corbyn's defeat was a Left which was demoralised, fragmented, disorganised and impotent. At the grassroots, activists were scattered and stopped in their tracks by Covid. Attempts to reconvene the fragments into a movement – such as the Enough Is Enough campaign, born of the 2022 summer of strikes and Mick Lynch mania – went nowhere. Meanwhile, any Labour backbencher who had the temerity to champion the party's supposed values (by, say, voting against keeping children in poverty) was stripped of the whip.

It is in this context that Zack Polanski was propelled to the leadership of the Green Party of England and Wales on a landslide 85 per cent of the membership's vote, in what was by far the most high-profile leadership race the party has ever run. The reasons for the high support and high public and media interest are on the face of it fairly obvious. Through the decade so far, millions of people who demonstrably support a leftwing break from the Thatcherite settlement have gone without representation while the cost-of-living crisis dominated (and, in many cases, ruined) their lives. As Labour tacked right and Reform UK hoovered up support, acres of political space opened up for a voice in mainstream politics to give this constituency what it lacked: hope.

Running on an insurgent programme of "eco-populism", Polanski's leadership bid echoed something of the mood of the campaign which carried Corbyn to lead Labour a decade earlier. Thousands of people were inspired to join the party and vote for Polanski. Press coverage and Google searches for the Green Party were unprecedented. And his first year of leadership transcended the wildest expectations of his supporters: quadrupling the party membership, doubling its polling, winning its first ever parliamentary by-election to return a fifth MP, and delivering the Greens' strongest ever set of local election results. "I want Starmer to be more afraid of losing votes and seats to the Greens than he is of losing them to Reform," Polanski said during his leadership campaign. True to his warning, Labour lost four times as many votes to the Greens than they did to Reform in the May 2026 elections.[6]

All of this has been in service of building a real alternative to social despair, economic decline and ecological collapse. That alternative is ecosocialism. Socialism has for centuries made the case for capitalism being responsible for the immiseration and exploitation of the working class. In addition to this traditional analysis, ecosocialists see capitalism – in its unending need to accumulate and grow – as the root cause of our ecological crisis, too, treating nature as both a free resource and a free rubbish dump. This system must be replaced with an economy under democratic control of ordinary people that operates for the common good rather than private profit. Critically, such an economy must exist within ecological limits. That means discarding both the profit motive and the pursuit of perpetual growth. The prize is a society which is abundant in the things that really matter: universal access to the fundamentals, a well-resourced public realm, a thriving civic life and much more free time. Also, not insignificantly, a liveable future on a habitable planet.

The lines between socialism and social democracy will be blurred in this book, just as they are in the practical politics of real life. In spite of the frothing protestations of our media class, what was put to the country in the 2017 Labour manifesto, for example, was not socialism but a radical social democracy – which is to say an interventionist state willing to tax, invest and regulate in the public interest. This is ultimately compatible with capitalism, rather than the decisive break offered by ecosocialism. It is helpful, however, to see the two philosophies on a spectrum, with the former as a staging post for the latter. There is no secret lever on the wall of 10 Downing Street labelled "socialism" which a prospective prime minister like Polanski could pull to transform society. Putting aside the possibility of violent revolution (which, as a study of the Green Party of England and Wales, this book does not consider), ecosocialism can only be realised through a process of social and political transition, strengthening social democratic principles which tend towards the eventual ability to transcend capitalism entirely. Therefore, whether we are taking practical steps towards robust social democracy or striding towards the glittering horizon of ecosocialism, the guiding political objective will be the same: displacing the centrality of the profit motive from our economy.

When Polanski first invoked the framing of the 99 per cent versus the 1 per cent during his leadership campaign, it felt almost anachronistic. Popularised during the Occupy movement which swept Western democracies in the aftermath of the 2008 financial crash, the slogan captured something of the sense of genuine possibility for transformative economic change alive at that moment of capitalist crisis. While the Occupy movement itself had no specific demands outside of a chaotic, quasi-anarchistic anti-capitalism, the resultant electoral surges for leftwing candidates across Western democracies offered countervailing visions for radical social democracy and socialism, from Jeremy Corbyn here in the UK to parties like Syriza and Podemos on the continent. In many cases this took the form of advocating specifically for green investment: rolling out renewable energy, insulating homes and restoring natural habitats.

All of this promise hit brick walls by the end of the 2010s. Movements calling for ambitious public investment in response to the 2008 crisis were overpowered by waves of austerity, under which most Western populations still gasp for air today. The fresh crises associated with Covid rekindled hope for an economic rethink and course correction, only for the promise to "build back better" to subside in the face of further divergence between rich and poor. By 2023, the "levelling up" agenda had openly given way to the then-prospective prime minister Rishi Sunak standing in front of Tory members in Tunbridge Wells and promising them a direct transfer of wealth to their area from poorer, urban communities.[7]

Given all this, it feels almost quaint to be reminded of the spirit of 2011 in 2026, back when we were unstoppable and another world was possible. But the framing of the 99 per cent versus the 1 per cent is even more relevant now than it was 15 years ago. Wealth inequality continues to widen. Over the past decade, the gap between the top and bottom 10 per cent has grown by 50 per cent.[8] Inequality is now a perennial problem in this country. The geographer Danny Dorling remembers decades spent arguing that the primary problem in this country wasn't poverty *per se* but inequality. "If 10 per cent of the population take 40 per cent of all income every year in the country, leaving 90 per cent on 60 per cent of income, you have a very, very divided society," he tells me. "This is very unusual compared to the rest of Europe. If you looked at other European countries you might wonder: why are they all living longer? Why are their cities neater? Why are their crime rates lower? Why are all their prisons less full?"

While a remote elite pulls away from the rest of society, living standards are declining for a growing number of people. Families which would have considered themselves to be affluent not all that long ago have been savaged by double-digit inflation and price gouging. The Resolution Foundation has calculated that the average family would today be £20,000 better off annually under the economic conditions of 20 years ago.[9] The Institute for Fiscal Studies reports that material deprivation shot up between 2019/20 and 2022/23. As a consequence of this, the number of people affected by food insecurity rose by almost half, and the number of people unable to heat their homes more than doubled.[10] Looking ahead, the Joseph Rowntree Foundation has predicted that all families will experience falling living standards by 2030, with lower income households falling twice as fast as middle and higher earners.[11] More and more people are struggling to make ends meet, or are no longer enjoying the standard of living to which they were previously accustomed. This means that the advancement of a leftwing politics which can command a social majority has rarely had a stronger grounding in people's material interests.

At the same time, Britain is fragmented like never before. This is most obviously on display in opinion polls regarding voting intention, demonstrating that – following some false dawns during the 2010s – we do now seem to be living in a genuinely multi-party political system. In the next general election, most voters face the prospect of going into a polling booth to cross their box on a ballot with up to five candidates with a credible chance of winning, forced through the funnel of first past the post (the non-proportional voting system used in the UK). Who can say what might come out the other end?

Labour and the Conservatives ended 2025 at an absolute nadir, both languishing at about 17 per cent in the polls.[12] Given how quickly seismic changes can embed themselves as the new normal, it's worth remembering what was relatively recently considered to be a crisis for these parties. When Labour MPs passed a motion of no confidence against Jeremy Corbyn in 2016, the party's polling had fallen to 33 per cent – a number Starmer could have only dreamed of in 2026, and which would have likely carried him to a comfortable second term. When ministers resigned en masse under Boris Johnson, the Conservatives had fallen to 30 per cent. These are figures not far off double what became normal for what we used to call the two big parties in the UK.

Underpinning this fragmentation is the murky and depressing psyche of a sharply atomised society increasingly dominated by the desperate, pessimistic and terminally online. The polling and research group More In Common has charted this terrain in their recent report, Shattered Britain, which outlines the extent to which a growing proportion of the public no longer believe the economy works in their interest and are willing to back insurgent outsiders promising to lay waste to the entire system.[13] In this respect Green voters and Reform voters share a key similarity. When asked to place themselves on a spectrum indicating their feelings about the dominant political institutions – over a fifth of voters for both parties choose "let them all burn". This compares with just 7 per cent for voters of both Labour and the Conservatives saying the same thing.[14] More In Common's report identifies a growing number of fault lines in public opinion which do not clearly map onto a traditional left–right spectrum, pointing towards a country of inchoate beliefs and values harnessed only when this widespread mistrust can be channelled into resentment.

The chief beneficiary of this fragmentation and crisis to date has been the far right. In electoral terms, that means Reform UK. Peaking in the polls in the mid-thirties over the summer of 2025, and remaining ahead ever since, their success can be attributed to three things: the talent of Nigel Farage, his ability to raise and weaponise the salience of migration, and the underlying (but unrelated) truth that people are completely within their rights to feel fed up and to want to see things changed.

The Labour government singularly failed to effectively arrest the rise of Reform in the polls. Indeed, they actively contributed to it. When faced with a vast bloc of voters for whom the salience of migration has been raised by reactionary forces, there are two conceivable broad strategies available to progressives: either make a proud, values-based counterargument in favour of the dignity of all people or work to lower the salience of the issue. Polanski gives a good go at both, defending the rights of migrants across the media while also trying to force the national conversation onto the terrain of inequality to be remedied by a wealth tax.

Labour, by contrast, attempted to chart a third way which could be described as the worst of all worlds: capitulating to the right on migration while ensuring the salience of the issue remains high. The strategy has been described as telling voters that Farage is right about everything – but don't vote for him![15] Labour has prior form on this. Perhaps most notable were the "controls on immigration" mugs ahead of the 2015 election that opened the door to a straightforward Conservative majority. But even in the 2000s, *Mail on Sunday* columnist Dan Hodges (then a member of Labour) chastised the party for kowtowing to British National Party (BNP) framing.[16] No lessons have been learnt. One consequence in September 2025 was the Unite the Kingdom march: one of the biggest far-right organised mobilisations in UK history, assembling some 150,000 people.

Pleased with the government's willingness to play its part in weaponising wedge issues, Reform UK cast around for other culture wars to stoke. Using the European Union (EU) referendum of 2016 as the blueprint, Farage's is the politics of the 50 per cent. Central to their political strategy is to find issues, like the question of whether to leave the EU or remain, which tear apart progressive coalitions and create a winner-takes-all fight to the death of two roughly equally sized camps, modelled on the hyper-sectarian polarisation of US politics.

In the years following 2016, the future Reform UK leader Richard Tice was the figurehead of a campaign to subject our net zero goals to a public referendum – an issue which, much like EU membership, hitherto enjoyed broad public and political consensus, and was of relatively low salience among the British people. More recently, they have even attempted to import the toxicity of the American debate around abortion to the UK, Farage meeting with anti-abortion lobbyists from the States and testing the waters of some public comments on the matter.[17] Unlike in America, Brits don't tend to conceptualise themselves as being "pro-life" or "pro-choice" akin to how we became conditioned to adopt wholesale identities around being "leave" or "remain". But creating new political subjects in this manner – divorced from material interests and class solidarity – is a key plank of Reform's evident strategy.

The vilest manifestation of this sort of politics was Reform's announcement of their policy to build detention centres in areas which vote Green.[18] Putting aside the nastiness (and the unworkability) of the policy, this represents a completely new form of politics in the UK: abandoning entirely any pretence of seeking to be a government for the whole country and openly promising to punish sections of the electorate once in office. To around half the country that might assemble within a socially progressive bloc of voters, they put up two fingers.

Our political landscape can be captured in these three percentages: 20 per cent, 50 per cent and 99 per cent. The 20 per cent represents the shattered fragments of the public, the rough level of support for most of the main parties, with these groups siloed by competing, calcifying values. If our election system is meant to produce a reflection of the will of the country, the combination of this fragmentation with first past the post will ensure that this reflection is distorted, potentially monstrously so. The 50 per cent is the politics of Farage and Reform, stoking culture wars to split progressive coalitions down the middle, polarising the population and radicalising their base.

The 99 per cent represents the utopian ambitions of a left-wing politics oriented towards building a social majority of shared interests. Polanski was right to evoke this old slogan in his leadership election. One of the clear political trends from the early 2010s until today is that there is a significant constituency in this country – from downwardly mobile graduates to immiserated public sector workers – which is attracted to socialist and radical social democratic reforms, and the conditions which give rise to this political desire are only becoming more pronounced. The political establishment is desperate to write off the result of the 2017 general election as a weird aberration. In an alternative telling, it was the opening chapter in a new political era, with almost all subsequent election results reassembling versions of two large blocs in the country: a reactionary right bloc and a left bloc agitating for a break from Thatcherism.

The ways in which the media class has contorted itself to disavow the reality of this progressive bloc in the electorate is staggering. The discourse around the politics of young people is instructive. Consider how many articles you have probably seen online about how young men are being drawn to the far right, often with implicit sympathy for their "legitimate concerns". In reality, support for Reform among young men is derisory. A YouGov poll from January 2026 found that Reform polls at 12 per cent among young men, relative to 30 per cent for the Greens.[19] Conversely, polling demonstrating that young women are exceptionally progressive – including on average having a more favourable view of communism than capitalism – was reported almost solely in terms of sexual moral panic. They won't have children! They're "driving men into the arms of cougars"! They're "angry young women"![20] What all this danced around was that nearly half of them are voting Green, but reactionary mainstream pundits can't bear to confer the party, or young women's opinions, with such legitimacy. Much better to dwell on their fertility.[21]

In the real world, the growing potential for assembling a social majority of voters around left politics has been well established over the last ten years. In Keir Milburn's *Generation Left*, he argues that "age has emerged as the key dividing line in politics. Young people are much more likely to vote Left and hold left-wing views while older generations are more likely to vote Right."[22] There is an age-old truism that people tend to be idealistic when young but swing right when they want governments to protect their accrued assets. However, the personal material improvements that lead to that switch are coming later in life or not all: home ownership, well-paid employment, a decent pension.[23] "As the Conservative support passes away," writes Phil Burton-Cartledge, "it is not replaced like for like by younger layers."[24] As was evidenced by the results of the May

2026 local elections, the Tories are now effectively a fringe party sustained by a cohort of property-owning pensioners in the south-east of England.

Polanski's first year of leadership has constituted a new battleground of British politics contested between the Greens and Reform. Following the Gorton and Denton by-election on 26 February 2026, the Greens came second in a national opinion poll for the first time in their history.[25] Similarly, following the May 2026 local elections, an extrapolated national result put Greens in second place.[26] On both occasions, Greens competed for first place with Reform, with the old duopoly in third and fourth places. As in so many places around the world, the centre has disintegrated, unable to deal with the weight of contradictions piled upon it by a political settlement which no longer delivers for most people. This is a moment of great peril but also great opportunity. While the country has never been so splintered, rarely have the structural conditions for building a majority of the Left ever been so ripe.

This book tells the story of how Zack Polanski was propelled to the leadership of the Green Party of England and Wales at this extraordinary political juncture, and argues that the Greens can be a vehicle for transformational politics in the years ahead – including playing a role in blocking a far-right government from sweeping to power in the general election of 2029.

Part I of this book charts the rise of the Greens in reverse chronological order. Chapter 1 chronicles the victory of the Greens in the historic Gorton and Denton by-election, reconfiguring the political landscape in Britain forever. Chapter 2 looks at Polanski's leadership campaign, explaining how he won his overwhelming mandate from the party membership. Chapter 3 contextualises Polanski's leadership in the party's recent past, told through the principled anti-austerity stance taken through the long 14 years of Conservative rule from 2010 to 2024. Chapter 4 goes back to the beginnings of the party, arguing that the potential for a politics like Polanski's has been encoded into the DNA of the party from its inception.

Part II of the book takes a more thematic overview of some of the tensions and contradictions within the party, demonstrating that they are either misunderstood or can be transcended through Polanski's leadership. Chapter 5 tackles the accusation that the Greens aren't really leftwing. Chapter 6 considers the potential tension between appealing to both urban and rural voters. Chapter 7 discusses the question of whether the party should focus solely on elections or wider organising. Finally, Chapter 8 explores the perceived trade-offs between people and planet, and how reconciling these priorities is the key to a political offer which can build a social majority.

There is much confusion about the nature of Zack Polanski and the Green Party of England and Wales. Critics from the left accuse the Greens of being Tories on bikes, and detractors from the right accuse Polanski of overseeing a far-left coup of an organisation imagined to be as politically supine as a village summer fair. The reality is that the Greens have a long, proud and principled history of leftwing politics, offering a unique critique of industrial capitalism and advocating for a radical vision of a fairer society on a safer planet. Rather than being some aberrative deviation from the party's past, this book suggests that

Polanski is instead the natural culmination of the history of the Green Party so far.

In his leadership campaign, Polanski pledged to make hope normal again. His first year has made good on that promise for millions of people, revitalising a broad and diverse British Left which desperately needed such an infusion of hope. Now we must take seriously the question of how we can actualise the social majority for leftwing transformation, which currently exists only in principle. That is to say: how do we move from the world of the 20 per cent to a world of the 99 per cent? Much has already been achieved. In sending Hannah Spencer to Parliament following the Greens' first ever parliamentary by-election victory, the stranglehold of the two-party duopoly has been loosened. In the May 2026 local elections, the Greens have swept Labour away in former heartlands like the London boroughs of Hackney and Lambeth. The party is now a viable and permanent electoral force, and Polanski has been tenacious in pursuit of maximising its vote across the country.

Less welcome facts nonetheless assert themselves. Most obviously that Reform – despite falling from their peak in the polls and underperforming in the local elections relative to dizzying expectations – are still in a strong position to form the next government. Tony Benn famously said that there is no final victory, nor final defeat. But few defeats will feel as final as the authoritarian reforms which will sweep the nation should Farage get the keys to 10 Downing Street. Climate commitments will be torn asunder. Minorities will be persecuted. Vast swathes of wealth will be transferred into fewer and fewer hands. And there will be little realistic prospect of resisting or reversing any of it before another general election.

Using Reform's peak as a working example, it would appear that the ceiling for any given party under present conditions is around a third of the electorate. The results of the local elections of May 2026 do not point to the Greens' ability to – by themselves – transcend this and translate a prospective social majority into an actual electoral majority. While Greens predictably surged in graduate-rich cities and continued to grow in rural areas too, Reform cut through the post-industrial towns of the North of England like a hot knife through butter – Labour losing every single councillor up for election in Wigan, for example, with Farage's outfit picking up 24 seats from a baseline of zero.[27] Rarely did the Greens meaningfully outperform in truly unexpected places.

This raises questions with no easy answers. Halfway between general elections, and with shuffling around at the top of the governing Labour Party, two things suggest themselves. Firstly, the Greens must see themselves as part of a wider ecology on the left, assuming shared responsibility for a project which goes beyond electoralism: reconstituting working-class consciousness and power and building that social majority for leftwing transformation outside of narrow party loyalty. Secondly, there must be serious thought about the realistic parliamentary arithmetic which returns a progressive government, blocking Farage from 10 Downing Street. This will call upon the Greens to draw upon their proud tradition of pluralism. Of course, the prospect of an outright Green majority might yet produce itself before 2029. Never say never. But more likely is that – whoever ends up leading Labour into the next election – this fragmentation of the electorate will persist into the next Parliament, if not forever.

All possibilities must be considered and prepared for. Nobody can confidently predict what will happen in the years ahead. One thing we do know for sure, however, is that the British Left is in a much-recovered strategic position relative to even just a couple of years ago. Today, in Polanski's Greens, we are presented with a vehicle for a broad coalition of progressives to arrest the advance of extreme rightwing politics, from the grassroots of our communities to the corridors of Parliament. This is cause for real hope. Hope alone will of course do nothing to loosen the grip of capital nor defeat the far right, but it is a precondition of the action required to win. So permit yourself to feel this unfamiliar feeling. It's time to rebuild the 99 per cent.

Part I

1

The Fifth Green MP

If the election of Zack Polanski as leader of the Green Party of England and Wales caused a political earthquake, the result of the Gorton and Denton by-election of February 2026 was the moment that the establishment parties were forced to look down at the chasm which had opened beneath their feet. Their voter base had gone. Nothing held them up but air.

In an election judged to be a three-way race between Labour, Reform and the Greens, the local plumber Hannah Spencer ended up running away with the contest on 41 per cent of the vote. Labour were beaten into third place. The Conservatives lost their deposit with just 706 people putting a cross in their box. The Greens and Reform gobbled up nearly 70 per cent of the vote between them – a proportion of the vote enjoyed by Labour alone as recently as 2019.[28] This represented only the second time Labour or the Tories had failed to take first or second place in the race for a parliamentary seat since 1945.[29] As the dawn broke over Manchester, Polanski and Spencer stood for photos for the press, her hand held aloft in victory. Neither Farage nor Starmer were anywhere to be seen.

The first ever parliamentary by-election win for the Green Party of England and Wales capped off an astonishing first few months under fresh leadership, and a decisive new chapter in a country where two-party politics was being torn asunder. Between September 2025 and February 2026, average national polling figures for the Greens roughly doubled, the membership quadrupled and a fifth MP was propelled to Parliament. When it comes to what a new leader has delivered for their party in their first six months, modern British politics offers no obvious parallels with what was achieved by Zack Polanski.

Who is Zack Polanski? In the middle of 2025, as his leadership campaign thrust him and the Greens into the spotlight, this was a question being asked by thousands of people for the first time. In the mouths of confused pundits and the political opponents who underestimated him, the question was witheringly sarcastic. Among many of the millions of ordinary people who had been starved of political representation by a Labour Party which had become, even in the words of the *Telegraph* columnist Tim Stanley, "the most rightwing government of my lifetime", it was a question asked with some earnest and excited curiosity.[30] Perhaps the menu of political options was about to broaden.

Polanski was born in 1982 and given the name David Paulden. He later restored his original familial name, which had been changed by his grandparents owing to the threat of antisemitic persecution. The forename Zack was taken from a character from *Goodnight Mister Tom*, chosen in part to differentiate himself from his stepfather, who was also named David. He is private about his background and family life, alluding to political disagreements with the more religious and conservative close relatives who feature among his immediate family. His partner Richie, however, appears across social media and speeches – as well as frequently being by Polanski's side in real life to support him through the stress of waiting for election results and to share in celebrating their outcomes. Polanski is an actor by background – widely considered to be one of the main reasons he is such a lauded communicator – along with having done all sorts of other jobs, too, from handing out yogurt samples to working the doors at the famous London nightclub Heaven. His work history includes, most notoriously, a stint as a hypnotherapist, which ended up in the pages of the *Sun* in 2013, where Polanski was the subject of a news story by a journalist who sought to increase her breast size via hypnotherapy. The rightwing media has also famously hung question marks over some parts of his CV: alleging that he has exaggerated roles with the Red Cross and the Ministry of Justice (with which he hosted fundraisers and worked for an agency providing training, respectively).[31]

If Polanski's professional life was varied, the same could be said for his political career to date. He speaks openly about coming to party politics relatively late in life, citing his earliest overt politicisation as the product of his experience with Theatre of the Oppressed, a form of leftist community theatre which includes the spectators as participants, inviting them to explore themes of power and collective agency. His work often actively included the experiences of marginalised people such as asylum seekers and sex workers. On one occasion, as an audience member, he saw an actor being rugby tackled by a participant, so overcome were they by their new sense of power.

Polanski's first formal involvement with party politics was to join the Liberal Democrats in 2015. He sought to stand as a candidate for the seat of Richmond Park in West London for a by-election in 2016 but was denied on the basis that the party resolved to shortlist only candidates who lived in the constituency – meaning the seat was to be contested and won by Sarah Olney, the only qualifying person who put herself forward. Videos of Polanski on stage at a Liberal Democrat conference during this period are now widely circulated by Labour as attack content. Polanski attributes his disenchantment with the record of the Liberal Democrats to political education: once he was exposed to the argument that the national economy is not like a household budget, the logic of austerity began to unravel for him. Other party positions, such as support for bombing Syria, also ushered him towards the exit. He then joined the Greens in 2017, not without suspicion from some London Greens who noted that the timing came very shortly after his path with the Liberal Democrats was blocked in Richmond. This suspicion was compounded when it transpired that he had not disclosed the notorious *Sun* article before being selected for the Green Party's list for the 2020 London Assembly elections. Such voices were swiftly silenced by his talents as a communicator and evident commitment to the party's success.

Today, Polanski is most frequently compared to the politicians Jeremy Corbyn and Nigel Farage: the former as a parallel, the latter as a populist mirror image. In this regard, the other two men share a similarity which Polanski does not: they have been unchanging over time. For decades, Corbyn and Farage's views and political positions have been fixed: Corbyn unwavering in his commitment to radical social democracy; Farage undertaking a decades-long crusade to realise a small state Britain outside of the European Union. In the last ten years alone, Polanski has been on a journey from praising the so-called accomplishments of the 2010–2015 Conservative–Lib-Dem coalition government on the stage of a Liberal Democrat conference to being a self-described socialist leader of the Greens. Now positioned as the only real rival to Farage, he is in one specific way more similar to Keir Starmer: a relative newcomer to the frontlines of party politics.

That said, from some of the discussion about him during the leadership election of 2025, you would think he had fallen from the sky the day before he announced his candidacy. Frequently described as a "surprise" entrant to the race, he was in fact the sitting deputy leader at the time and thereby precisely the sort of person you would very much expect to take a tilt at the top job. He had held a number of public-facing roles over his eight years in the party prior to that. Even with the relatively low-profile brief of spokesperson for democracy, he was able to evidence the raw materials of being one of the best communicators the Greens had to offer. Winning a seat on the London Assembly followed in 2021 before his election to deputy of the party the year after.

It was from these positions that Polanski was able to develop his appeal to the wider membership: demonstrating his ability to hold the mayor of the capital city to account; excelling in higher-profile media interviews; and travelling the country by train to go door-knocking with local parties. Paying due deference to grafting in the party's ground game (activists campaigning for local candidates door to door) while giving members a small taste of how he could electrify their air game (the national media campaign), Polanski was laying the foundations for a leadership contest which would change everything. In the spring of 2025 he announced his candidacy, kicking off a frenzy of media attention for Polanski and the Greens which will be explored in more detail in Chapter 2. In that September, he was elected leader on an unprecedented mandate from the party membership.

Predictions that the spotlight on Polanski would be unplugged when the media circus moved on following the leadership election proved to be wrong. If anything, the momentum behind Polanski's leadership accelerated. While a few thousand new members joined during the leadership election in order to vote for him, the platform earned by his election resulted in a complete explosion of tens of thousands of new members. Media appearances did not dry up but grew in stature. Polanski proved himself adept at handling both hostility on the couch of BBC's *Sunday with Laura Kuenssberg* and bawdy comedy on the sofa of Friday night's *The Last Leg* on Channel 4. Making a sly reference to the notorious hypnotherapy story, the comedian Alex Brooker (who has congenital deformities) jokingly asked if he could increase the size of his hands. "That's not the body part you were asking about backstage," came Polanski's reply. Not since Jeremy Corbyn sat on the *One Show* sofa talking about jam and allotments had a leftist politician seemed so at ease with themselves on a light entertainment show.

One of the most striking moments in the early weeks of Polanski's leadership was his debut appearance on BBC's *Question Time*, in October 2025, going head-to-head with Reform's head of policy and spokesperson for home affairs, Zia Yusuf, alongside MPs from Labour and the Conservatives. Two related things stood out from the performance. The first was the heated combativeness between Polanski and Yusuf. Polanski went in hard on the issue of former Welsh Reform leader Nathan Gill's conviction for taking bribes from pro-Russian politicians and branded Reform's programme as "fascism". Yusuf for his part fired the starting pistol on a new world of scrutiny and attack of Green policy positions, claiming Polanski wanted open borders and completely legalised drugs, as well as reminding the audience about his past as a hypnotherapist.

For many of Polanski's actual and potential supporters, it was a dream come true to finally see a frontline politician go toe to toe with an insurgent far right which they felt had not been adequately neutered by a Labour government. Others worried that this attack came at the expense of promoting the Greens' positive and popular vision for society: Polanski swinging too hard and punching air. Whichever interpretation viewers favoured, all of this was to highlight the second and perhaps even more striking thing about *Question Time*: the utter irrelevance of the Labour and Conservative figures on the panel – the names of whom would have been forgotten by viewers by the next morning – sitting mutely while the representatives of Reform and Greens engaged in what was at times effectively a head-to-head debate. This in a one-hour microcosm laid out the new contours of English politics: the legacy parties falling into the abyss while insurgent parties to the left and right hoovered up support and set the stage for the real contest of the next electoral cycle.

Against this backdrop of the marginalisation of the main parties, Polanski strengthened the position of the Greens week by week with a growing membership and a series of high-profile defections and acquisitions. The former Labour MP Lloyd Russell-Moyle announced that he had joined the Greens in November 2025, in a press conference alongside Polanski. He was now presumed to seek a mandate from local members to run for the Greens in the place of his former constituency (now Brighton Kempton and Peacehaven after the boundary review) in the next general election. Another notable acquisition followed in January 2026 in the form of Mish Rahman, a former member of Labour's National Executive Committee (NEC). Backed by a faction of Momentum, he had narrowly failed to be re-elected in 2024 and quit the party in 2025 vowing to "remove [Labour] from power".[32]

Perhaps the highest profile of these moments was the quasi-defection of Jamie Driscoll from his association with the Your Party project, where he was a director of the company which had been set up to manage the provisional party's data and funds, before resigning and entrusting it to Zarah Sultana in October 2025. Having never actually joined Your Party after it was constituted, Driscoll joined the Greens in December. Aside from what this signalled about the position of the Greens relative to Corbyn and Sultana's fledgling efforts to create a mass party of the Left, Driscoll also came with the credibility of a person who had exercised a significant amount of state power as the former mayor of the North of Tyne Combined Authority. There are not many figures in British politics who can blend a good track record of delivery at municipal level with genuine leftwing credentials, but Driscoll is among them. Having been blocked in 2023 from re-running for mayor as a Labour candidate, he founded the organisation Majority – a membership organisation advocating for a progressive alliance, backing aligned candidates from a range of parties and none. Here again was someone committed to reconstituting the politics of the 99 per cent, on a popular policy platform which could build common ground.

While Reform arguably diluted their insurgent character by welcoming in more and more washed-up Tories from the Johnson and Truss eras, Polanski was bringing in people with real moral authority and practical political experience. Most critically, such figures had not been tarnished by association with Starmer's Labour. Tory escapees to Reform could not free themselves of a similar stain. After a Reform Party conference was criticised for giving platforms to cranks and vaccine deniers, Farage hoped that these defections would help Reform look like a government in waiting – as he continued the high-wire act of insurgency and credibility which he has had to constantly walk. Instead, it made Reform look like a government the country had already thrown out. There is an obvious political tension in weaponising the "Boris Wave" of immigration among your voter base while bringing in a slew of ex-ministers who oversaw it. This tension was not adequately resolved. The fall from their peak in the polls quickly followed.

Everything on the dashboard was displaying a good reading when it came to Polanski's leadership pitch to the membership being put into practice: the clear political positioning and heightened media attention was giving rise to higher polling numbers, a swelling membership, and a steady stream of defections from Labour councillors and other notable figures from the Left. There was, however, one further bridge to cross in order to be fully vindicated in the eyes of his critics. Their central question and challenge remained: could this all translate into a step change of electoral success? Early in 2026, this question would be answered. It would also end up taking the Greens a step closer to the goal which Polanski had set for his own leadership: to replace Labour.

The by-election of Gorton and Denton was triggered by the resignation of the MP Andrew Gwynne, who had been sitting as an independent after he was suspended from the Labour Party in February 2025 for sending offensive WhatsApp messages. Immediately the character of this contest took on existential proportions for Starmer's premiership. It had long been an open secret that discussions were underway to quietly find a way for the mayor of Greater Manchester, Andy Burnham, to return to Parliament for the purpose of challenging Starmer's leadership from the soft-left. In addition to that, the national poll ratings of the incumbent government and the insurgent parties to its left and its right meant that this would be the first real test of how Labour would perform in a parliamentary contest now that it had shed support in both directions, especially since the election of Polanski to leader. For both Starmer and Labour more broadly, this election raised real questions of survival.

This was not a high priority seat for the Greens, sitting at 127th on its target list, as listed by the swing which would be required to win. Away from these raw numbers based on the

Greens' electoral track record to date, nor was it in profile an obvious fit for the specific positioning of Polanski's leadership, articulating a politics which was of highest natural appeal among downwardly mobile graduates in the sort of inner-city constituencies which formed the overwhelming majority of the 39 second-place positions achieved in the 2024 general election. Instead, Gorton and Denton, as a constituency, was a weird, distorted product of the 2023 boundary review, drawing a border which looked kind of like a sagging bow tie, two big and very different areas pinched and joined in the middle.

Overall, the constituency is 57 per cent white, and Asians make up just over a quarter of the population.[33] This is not evenly distributed between the titular names of the constituency. The town of Denton – which Reform saw as their route to victory – is 90 per cent white. Almost all of the constituency's Muslim community is concentrated in a small area of Gorton called Longsight. The constituency as a whole is significantly more deprived than any of the four seats currently held by Greens.[34] In short, this was in microcosm a test of Polanski's ability to keep alive the claim that the Greens' ground game can win anywhere.

The tight timelines imposed by Labour forced the Greens to make a snap decision about whether to go all in on Gorton and Denton or to effectively sit it out. Within 24 hours of the date of the by-election being set – and before the field of candidates had been established – the party resolved to throw the kitchen sink at this by-election and set into motion the necessary internal processes to move ahead and begin building local campaigning infrastructure. The aspiration to return a fifth MP to Parliament before the next general election had been established at the party's autumn conference of 2024, and this opportunity had to be taken. As more details of the race solidified, the Greens fancied their chances all the more.

The candidates who didn't run were almost as important as the ones who did. In a short-sighted tactical move, responsive purely to the crisis of the day, as was increasingly emblematic of Starmer's leadership, the prime minister personally intervened in an NEC vote to help ensure that Burnham was prevented from running.[35] In doing so, he blocked the only candidate who had any shot of holding the seat for Labour. Their eventual candidate, a local councillor named Angeliki Stogia, survived the contest without making any meaningful impression upon public consciousness. From the moment Burnham was blocked, a loss to the Greens or Reform was near enough guaranteed and the longer-term political damage to the governing party was all the greater.

The other major candidate who wasn't actually on the ballot paper was Polanski himself. As soon as the by-election was called, speculation mounted that Polanski must be tempted to have a crack at it. Polanski, though, quickly ruled this idea out on the grounds that the candidate should be local and, despite the fact he was originally from Manchester, he confirmed that he had his eye on a London seat in the next general election, where he had lived for about 20 years. One could speculate about two further reasons. Firstly, Polanski likely recognised the diminishing effect it would have had for him to be shackled to Westminster, and the political class against which he was so effectively rallying across the country. Better to preserve the freedom to travel and campaign, untarnished by the institutionalising effect becoming an

MP would unavoidably have. Secondly, Polanski has shown himself to be deft at putting himself forward for races he had high confidence he could win. To lose a by-election so soon after taking the leadership would crush the credibility he had so quickly built. With the information available at the moment he had to decide, this was not a risk worth taking.

In the end, the actual candidates in the race turned out to be incredibly emblematic of the wider political trends they represented. For the Greens, selected by her local party with an overwhelming mandate was the plumber and trainee plasterer Hannah Spencer. She was a relatively new member of the party, who had joined in 2022 but quickly ascended to prominence by becoming local councillor for Hale on Trafford Council in 2023 and spokesperson for refugee and migration in 2025. As a straight-talking, white working-class Mancunian woman rooted in the community, she was the pitch-perfect choice of candidate to face up to Reform, pushing back on far-right rhetoric while visibly being of the demographic to which they were trying to appeal. A genuinely likeable character, Spencer is in a minority of one among MPs whom you actually believe when they say they could murder a Greggs sausage roll.

Reform, by contrast, chose the most alienating candidate imaginable. Matt Goodwin was formerly an academic recognised for writing *about* the far right who had, over time, become a radicalised member *of* the far right himself, platforming replacement theory poison and presenting his own show on GB News. Not only did he not live in Manchester, disparaging past remarks were quite quickly uncovered, with Labour circulating a clip of him confiding to a public audience that he had been "unfortunate enough to be in Manchester a few days ago".[36] The gifted framing of the election being "grafter versus grifter" was seized upon by the Greens with relish. The stage was set for what the prime minister quite accurately called a battle "for the soul of the nation", but it was one in which Labour would turn out to be a bit player.

As soon as the election was called, it was immediately framed as a three-way race between Labour, Reform and the Greens – the former as the *de facto* incumbent (the area held by Labour for over 90 years) with the latter two as serious contenders from either side. From the start, the Greens believed the seat to be winnable on paper but never allowed themselves to believe victory was a certainty.

"When the early canvassing returns came it looked OK," remembers head of elections Chris Williams.

> Then throughout there was this whole list of things that just swung momentum our way: Burnham being blocked. Hannah being selected. The response from the membership was so positive. The fundraising emails were record-breaking for us. The media narrative was shifting. The bookies put us as favourites early on. Two independent polls came out saying we could win. The vibes we were getting on the ground were that the energy was with us, and people *wanted* us to win.

With this momentum building, the question of tactical voting and calls for collaboration across the Left loomed large in the contest. The Workers Party (the controversial leftist party fronted by George Galloway, with strong socially regressive tendencies) responded to this by stepping aside, freeing up the 10 per cent of the vote they achieved in 2024 (a number which might reasonably be expected to have climbed modestly against Labour's fall) to transfer in bulk to the Greens. The socialist paper the *Morning Star* endorsed a Green candidate for the first time in its history. The Grassroots Left faction of Your Party (associated with Sultana) distinguished itself by outrightly refusing to endorse Spencer, to the widespread dismay of almost everyone else on the Left; however, to his credit, Corbyn himself eventually explicitly backed the Green candidate.

Increasingly, it was becoming possible to invert the Labour attack line that voting Green would let in Reform. A lower profile by-election at local authority level evidenced this a week or so before the parliamentary by-election. In Fletton and Woodston, Greens surged by 16 per cent to a 28 per cent total, while Labour cascaded from 48 per cent to 17 per cent, putting them in fourth place behind the Tories. Reform – who had not stood previously – took 29 per cent of the vote, which was enough for them to come through the middle and win a seat with nearly 20 per cent fewer percentage points than its winner achieved last time. This was the risk of a fragmented politics under first past the post written in miniature. Of course, a single council ward in Petersham was by no means a good predictor for the results in Gorton and Denton, but as a harbinger of what the country could wake up to, it was to focus minds. The Greens had to storm this. If it provoked any soul searching within Labour themselves, however, it was not discernible from their campaign, which went on claiming that a vote for the Greens risked letting in Reform, in contradiction to available polling and recent results.

In parliamentary by-elections, Greens have tended to operate with the sort of anonymity now reserved for Conservative candidates. Indeed, Spencer had run in recent elections to typical levels of Green success for non-target seats: finishing fifth in the 2024 Greater Manchester mayoral race and fourth in her 2024 general election contest. All of this was to change under the leadership of Zack Polanski, and the prevailing conditions of political realignment. Once the bookies named the Greens as nailed on favourites early in the contest, the smears which descended upon Hannah and the party confirmed her as being understood to be a truly serious contender. Many of them were borderline funny: the *Daily Mail*'s best efforts being to dredge up a holiday she'd taken by plane about ten years ago and a picture of her standing next to (someone else's) non-electric car, marshalled as evidence of savage hypocrisy. Others pointed to the fact that she had installed heat pumps as proof of the fact that she was somehow not *really* a plumber but in fact extremely woke and posh.

Not all the dirty tactics were so frivolous, however. In response to publishing campaign material in Urdu, accusations of sectarianism escalated to the point that it was implied that directly communicating with residents about their actual concerns was to be viewed as somehow illegitimate. Photographs of Starmer fraternising with Netanyahu were said to be weaponised. How this was to be squared with Labour figures' repeated insistence that issues like Gaza did not pass the lips of anyone they met on the doorsteps was never made clear. At the moment that polls closed, accusations were raised of a practice known as "family voting", whereby more than one person went into the booth at the same time. (The implication, here, was that the votes of Muslim women and families were being cast at the behest of a patriarch.) The returning officer noted that not only had no polling station staff reported this but such concerns should have been raised while the practice was happening so that it could have been stopped. Following the result, the response from Farage and Goodwin descended to allegations of "cheating", which barely stopped short of saying that it would have been fairer if Muslims weren't allowed to vote at all.[37] At the end of March, following a police investigation, it was concluded that there was "no evidence" of the alleged family voting.[38]

Meanwhile, the outrightly dishonest campaigning tactics of an increasingly desperate Labour aroused far less outcry. The most notable was the delivery to voters of leaflets which claimed that an organisation named Tactical Choice recommended that voters who wanted to block Reform ought to vote Labour. Scandalously, no such organisation existed.[39] Contrasting with the endless pontification about so-called sectarianism, this straightforward deception passed almost without comment in the mainstream media. In reality, all the credible tactical voting platforms recognised and endorsed Greens as the party best placed to defeat Reform. This election turned into a dry run of what the result ensured would become a permanent mode of negative campaigning for a Labour newly challenged from its left: focussing on a distortion of drugs and sex work policies built on the principles of harm reduction which rendered them as an active desire to turn playgrounds into crack dens.

Labour would have known perfectly well that such campaigning risked confusing and splitting the anti-Reform vote and letting Goodwin through the middle. Why would they do this?

Many speculated that despite Labour's stated claim that stopping Reform was the primary objective of their campaign, they privately believed that a Green win would be the real disaster. The political reason for this was clear: losing a seat to Reform and being able to blame the Greens for splitting the vote was infinitely preferable to a Green victory which demonstrated that Labour was not the only – or even primary – party capable of locking Farage out of 10 Downing Street at the next general election. This was the only card they had left to play with regard to rebuilding any winning national voting coalition. The actual result – coming third behind Reform – was a nightmare that endured for Labour beyond the daybreak of Friday 27 February. As with the blocking of Burnham from running for the seat in the first place, Starmer had once again subordinated all wider political goals to the preservation of his premiership. Sending to Parliament a man who obsesses over the demographic breakdown of Britons by skin colour would have been a price worth paying.

One of the most notable facets of the campaign was the difference made by the massively increased membership of the Green Party of England and Wales. The open space of the local Greenbank Lane Park was used as a meeting point to accommodate the hundreds of people who routinely turned up to canvas, many of them for the first time. Novara Media's Aaron Bastani tweeted a picture of the Green Party HQ heaving with activists, saying it looked more like a kebab shop in Shoreditch at 2 A.M. An Instagram video showed 300 people in a hall who had turned up to address tens of thousands of envelopes by hand. And polling day saw what was widely recognised as being possibly the most sensational ground campaign of any by-election in British history. Around 2,000 people turned up to get the vote out for the Greens, knocking on doors, delivering leaflets and knocking doors again.

Campaign organisers remember people queuing up outside the office from 6 A.M. ready to go leafleting. They split signed-up volunteers into 70 teams covering all the wards of the constituency but still had people just turning up on the day – more than they needed. It meant they were able to do things they wouldn't normally do on a polling day, like leafleting outside school gates at the end of lessons, and outside mosques at the end of prayers. They even ended up sending out some "cheer squads": groups of people with Vote Green signs playing music and dancing at busy road intersections and similar spots. People who had been teamed up with random strangers at the start of the day returned to Green Party HQ as friends.

This was the culmination of a people-powered campaign flooded with optimism and hope. While activists literally danced through the streets in the rain, and the deputy leader Mothin Ali crowdsurfed over volunteers at a party blaring some of Hannah's speeches set to drum and bass, Labour put forward figures like Luke Akehurst MP to keep peddling the threadbare nonsense that only their party was in contention to defeat Reform. While this happened, more and more canvassers on the ground reported that swathes of undecideds were breaking for the Greens. "In the final days, we saw the data improving so much more," remembers Chris Williams. "Even then we still said: let's just not believe it. Because it was just so much better than what was showing up in the polls. We thought there must be some sort of mistake." There was no mistake.

By 3 A.M. on Friday, it would be down to the justifiably miserable-looking Labour deputy leader Lucy Powell to explain to the viewers of BBC News how they had managed to come third in what they had insisted was a two-horse race. An hour or so later, Zack Polanski and Hannah Spencer entered the count together, shortly before the returning officer took to the stage to deliver the results. The victory speech which Spencer delivered blended hopeful optimism with the anger that ordinary people felt as a result of falling living standards and a failing political class. She said:

> Working hard used to get you something. It got you a house. A nice life. Holidays. It got you somewhere.
>
> But now – working hard? What does that get you? Because talk to anyone here and they'll tell you. The people who work hard but can't put food on the table. Can't get their kids school uniforms. Can't put their heating on. Can't live off the pension they worked hard to save for. Can't even begin to dream about ever having a holiday. Ever. Because life has changed.
>
> Instead of working for a nice life, we're working to line the pockets of billionaires. We are being bled dry. I don't think it's extreme or radical to think working hard should get you a nice life. And if you're not able to work, you should still have a nice life. I think that absolutely everybody should get a nice life.[40]

Here was the rebuilding of the 99 per cent, speaking to the majority of people with the common experience of their lives getting worse, while wealth gets hoovered up by a vanishingly small number of people. Spencer named enemies while building a broad coalition. She had learned from the success of Polanski's political positioning, which had reached millions: meeting people's anger but directing it towards hope and the restoration of the belief that politics could actually change your life for the better.

Her unique additional quality was to be unconditionally representative of the British working class, and with a waver still present in her public-speaking voice, unmistakably removed from the professional, careerist political class. She spoke to the regular indignity and humiliation suffered by millions of people "looked down on" by our establishment, "maybe because we didn't do well at school, maybe because we do dirty, manual jobs". Apologising to her customers whose work she had to cancel on account of having to head to Westminster, she promised that, "when I get there, I will make space for everyone doing jobs like mine. We will finally have a seat at the table."[41]

It's difficult to overstate how extraordinary was the achievement of Spencer and Polanski in Gorton and Denton. The final polling ahead of the election put the Greens on 30 per cent among people likely to vote.[42] The actual result was more than ten points clear of that, quadrupling their previous by-election best of 10.2 per cent.[43] In doing so, they overturned the seventh-largest Labour majority ever toppled in a by-election, and the third-largest this century. Their 27.5 per cent swing represents the biggest vote increase the Greens have ever registered in a by-election – knocking into second place a somewhat more modest 5.1 per cent.[44] This wasn't just scraping over the line to win their first ever parliamentary by-election. This was something else entirely.

It's important to temper these transports of joy among Green activists and voters with a few persistent, sobering facts. The first is that, despite it being an emphatic Green victory, it was by no means a bad showing for Reform. They achieved a swing of 15 per cent and did so in a seat which was significantly lower on their target list than it was for the Greens. If this swing had been replicated in a general election, Reform would still come out as the largest party with 254 seats.[45] This is, of course, unlikely to happen given the unique nature of by-elections, which brings us on to the second grounds for caution for the Greens: it will be immensely difficult to replicate this success at scale, relying as it did on mobilising thousands of activists from across the country for a targeted, one-off event, which could not be relied upon in a general election where many seats will be fought at once. Finally, it would also be true to say that while Hannah Spencer was an exceptional candidate, she competed against the most favourable set of opponents imaginable. Given that Reform has both Muslims and people of colour among its most prominent politicians, quite why they chose such a uniquely aggravating figure for this constituency is puzzling. Similarly, Labour had access to one of the few candidates who had a shot at holding the seat for a government in freefall, but they chose to run a corporate lobbyist whom nobody had heard of. Greens cannot count on conditions being so favourable in future contests.

Still, this was a success without precedent in half a century of the Greens' existence. Hannah Spencer's election to Parliament encapsulated so many facets of the Greens under the leadership of Zack Polanski. It showed how a mobilised mass membership can be a difference maker when standing up to parties backed by billionaires. It proved that the party can go on winning in constituencies which aren't primarily populated by their typical base of supporters. And in sending a plumber to Parliament, it also offered further evidence of the party's changing class composition.

But as the pollster Luke Tryl noted on the morning of the result, this was above anything else concrete proof that the bounce that Polanski had provided for the party in the national polls was having observable effects on actual elections.[46] On BBC News, the legendary elections guru John Curtice said of the result that "there are particular elections we all remember ... This is going to be up with those in the history books and our political memory. This is a seismic event." The contours of politics in the UK had changed forever. Overnight, the prospect of a Reform-led government as the consequence of the 2029 general election felt a little less inevitable, to the relief of millions. For Labour, the result had existential implications: at her first press conference as MP, Spencer noted that there were no less than 126 seats which could be lost on a smaller swing to the Greens than they had achieved in Gorton and Denton.[47]

The week after the result, Sky News published new polling – conducted after Spencer's win – which put the Greens in their highest ever position: 21 per cent.[48] This was just two points behind Reform and knocked Labour into third by a clear five points. The argument that Greens were a wasted vote has been eviscerated, and another fragment of support to which Labour had clung on under that basis was lost. For years on end, polling had revealed the Greens' policy position to be the true preference of a significant proportion of voters. But many voters were held back by the barrier of believing the Greens couldn't win. This threshold had now been crossed decisively. A fifth MP and second place in the polls had been won within six months of taking leadership. Here was the Polanski effect in action.

2

The Polanski Effect

"I think we are extremely fortunate that the Green Party are shit," said an anonymous Labour minister in May 2025, mere days before Zack Polanski announced that he would be running to lead the Greens. "If they had any kind of charismatic or populist leadership, we'd be eight to ten points further down the polls."[49] As it turned out, the membership of the Green Party of England and Wales shared this view. Just a few months later, Polanski's populism and charisma propelled him to the leadership of the party on an unprecedented mandate of 85 per cent of the vote, a result rivalled only by Caroline Lucas when she was elected as the party's first ever leader in 2008.

The effect which Polanski had on the country surpassed even the wildest expectations of his campaign team. In the foothills of planning the leadership campaign, the team talked about 10,000 new members as a prospective "avalanche" and shied away from committing to pledges like doubling the membership by the time of the next general election for fear of raising expectations too high. In reality, Polanski nearly quadrupled the membership by Christmas. Regrettably, there is no recorded reaction to any of this from the anonymous Labour source.

From the outset of this astonishing campaign, swathes of commentators and critics painted Polanski's platform as a rupture from the tradition of the Greens and a battle for the soul of the party. In reality, he was as much a continuity candidate as he was a breath of fresh air, proudly articulating the settled politics of the Greens with conviction and without compromise. This, being a natural champion of the values and the policies of the party, is what ultimately carried him to victory among his membership over the summer of 2025. It also had an electrifying effect across the wider public. His candidacy evidenced all of the qualities he would embody as leader and put in place the political positioning which would shift the contours of British politics in rapid order. It was obvious to anyone with eyes to see that there was political space to be occupied to the left of Starmer's Labour. Few, however, could have predicted just how quickly and decisively the prospects for a radical political programme could be restored.

Polanski launched his campaign to be leader of the Green Party of England and Wales in a high-profile piece in the *Guardian* on 5 May 2025, mere days after local elections which had seen Reform win control of ten councils from a standing start. Both main parties had suffered heavy losses. Greens advanced, as they now always do in local elections, but with a much more modest 44 seats.[50] By any honest assessment, Reform was making the running.

Until around 2024, it was possible for people on the broad left of politics to tell themselves consoling stories about the true threat posed by the far right in electoral terms. For most of the 2010s, the Greens and the United Kingdom Independence Party (UKIP) gave representation to significant but minority constituencies of the public to the left and right of the larger two parties. But while UKIP had an ability to elect rafts of councillors by turning surges of national resentment into local electoral results, they just as quickly washed back out with the tide, usually either imploding in office or failing to be re-elected after demonstrating some combination of indifference or incompetence. After becoming England's fourth party of local government by the mid-2010s, UKIP suffered successive losses year on year until they were completely without representation by 2023.[51] For the first few years of its existence, the Brexit Party (later to be renamed Reform) got nowhere at local level. Greens, by contrast, tended to be re-elected, and grew in number at each election – dramatically so from 2019 onwards. The overall picture was one in which the Greens were more effectively building electoral power cumulatively, while far-right counterparts failed to capitalise on their polling numbers in the long term.

Reform eventually smashed these shibboleths to pieces, starting with the general election of 2024, in which they returned five MPs to Parliament, in comparison to the Greens' four. In six years, Reform had surpassed what the Greens had achieved in 60. By the start of 2025, Reform was comfortably and consistently polling well above 20 per cent, while the Greens languished well below 10 per cent, failing to convert its new national platform into higher national polling. It was still just about possible to tell oneself that national polling had little to say about how this would translate into electoral success under first past the post, but the local elections of May 2025 put paid to that. Reform won an astonishing 677 councillors from a baseline of none – not far off double that of the second-biggest winners, the Liberal Democrats, who won 370 seats.[52] One by one, the straws to which Greens could clutch were torn from their hands. We were living in a new political reality and despite the incredible breakthrough of quadrupling the Greens' number of MPs, it felt like the Left wasn't even on the pitch.

Naranee Ruthra-Rajan has been a member of the Green Party since 2009 and first met Polanski after being paired together to go leafleting during the 2019 European elections. She subsequently acted as his election agent in the 2019 general election and ran the campaign for his successful bid to become deputy leader in 2022. When she saw him around Christmas 2024, he wasn't sure that he wanted to go for the top job, especially without clarity on whether the incumbent co-leaders Ramsay and Denyer would run again. During another meeting in February, he seemed more sure. By March, "we were planning everything, writing strategy and sitting down and working out what our messaging could be", Ruthra-Rajan remembers. With the assembling campaign team catching wind that incumbent co-leader Adrian Ramsay was preparing to launch a bid, "we knew that if you announce your candidacy earlier, it can prevent other people from announcing, and so we wanted to do that", Ruthra-Rajan says. "But Zack was also quite persuasive about not wanting to mess up the May elections, so that's why we decided to launch straight after."

Polanski was the first to declare himself as standing in the race, with a rapid response to the drubbing that an insurgent far right had given a moribund establishment, and in doing so demonstrated two of his principal qualities: his ability to seize opportunities and grasp the initiative. Polanski used his interview in the *Guardian* to ring the alarm on the growing gulf between the Greens and Reform, noting that, while Green policies routinely poll strongly among the public, the gaps in everything from media visibility to party membership were shocking. Saying that the Left needed to learn from the tactical and strategic successes of a figure like Farage, Polanski argued that a programme of "eco-populism" was needed to ensure that the Greens achieved the platform they deserved. What did this look like? It involved communications which foregrounded policies that spoke to people's immediate, material needs; acknowledging and feeling the public's justified anger but directing it towards hope; shaping strong narratives with clear enemies; and building a mass party which was powered by a broader social base of vibrant movements. Farage was, in Polanski's view, first and foremost an exemplary storyteller. It was time for socialism to tell a new story of its own.

"I think the story we need to tell is one that connects with people, which is about food on the plate, heat in their homes, and for it to feel relevant to their everyday lives," Polanski explains. "What eco-populism was looking to do was to connect on an emotional level with the things people are worried about today, and then connect these things more widely with issues around the current crises in the economy and around the world."

Three days after Polanski launched his bid, one of the incumbent co-leaders, Carla Denyer, announced that she would not be re-running for the position, choosing instead to focus on her responsibilities as an MP for Bristol Central. Denyer had been elected as co-leader alongside Adrian Ramsay in 2021, and the subsequent contest in 2025 fell approximately a year after Denyer and Ramsay had been elected to Parliament. With Denyer choosing not to re-run for the leadership, Polanski's opponents took the form of Ramsay, who is MP for Waveney Valley, paired up with one of the other four Green MPs, Ellie Chowns, who represents Hereford North.

Ramsay has a long and high-profile history with the party, having served as deputy leader of the party to Caroline Lucas from 2008 to 2012. Chowns was elected as a councillor in 2017 and was subsequently elected as a member of the European parliament (MEP) in 2019. Both, crucially to the dynamics of this campaign, represented rural areas in which they had defeated incumbent Conservative MPs (contrasted to the other two Green seats which were won by overturning Labour majorities in urban constituencies). Their pitch to the membership from the outset defined the broad contours of the contest throughout: claiming that what the Green Party leadership requires is the credibility of parliamentarians and the track record of winning in hard-to-win places.

Their route to Parliament was undoubtedly impressive, both achieving swings of over 30 per cent to come from third and fourth places in 2019 to overturn Conservative majorities upwards of 20,000. This speaks to the strength of the Green Party's ground campaign and their unmistakable talents as local candidates in those seats. These qualities did, however, risk putting them slightly at odds with a more radical and urban party activist base, with the median member of the Greens far more naturally aligned to the style and political substance of the outgoing incumbent Denyer, more confidently speaking in the language of social justice, rights for minorities and climate as a class issue. It also ran somewhat against the implied electoral logic presented by the 39 constituencies in which the party came second place in the 2024 general election – overwhelmingly southern, urban constituencies demographically very similar to the Brighton and Bristol seats.

The central choice before the membership was set out from the beginning of the race: an outsider untainted by the trappings of a Westminster which the public despised, promising to build an insurgent mass movement that could replace Labour and defeat Reform, or a duo of MPs tethered between Whitehall and small-c conservative rural constituencies, promising steady-as-she-goes incrementalism which built on decades of unmistakable, but gradual, progress. At this point in the campaign, safe money would have been bet on this being a fairly close contest. Internal elections for the Green Party historically have extremely small turnouts from a relatively disengaged wider membership, and while the average member was likely to in principle be more impressed by Polanski's communications skills and politics, they were equally likely to be swayed by the prestige of the party's parliamentary team and inclined to stick with the incumbency of a leader, in Ramsay, who had overseen the breakthrough of going from one Green MP to four. Ramsay and Chowns also enjoyed the endorsement of much of what you might call the party establishment, most notably the beloved Caroline Lucas.

At the outset of the campaign, Polanski's team had split the membership into four broad camps. The first was young, ex-Corbyn supporters who left Labour for the Greens at some point between 2020 and the present moment, which were expected to overwhelmingly back Polanski. The second was the millennial cohort of those who joined during the anti-austerity Green surge of 2015, also judged to be extremely aligned to Polanski, if more protective of the hard-won glories resulting from the incrementalist march towards the parliamentary breakthrough over those ten years. The third was the wave of members who joined in response to Caroline Lucas' election to Parliament in 2010, again a broadly aligned group of people, albeit perhaps more inclined to value pluralism and consensus building as virtues unto themselves, and slightly turned off by the outright class antagonism implicit within Polanski's pitch. The fourth, and judged to be hardest to win over, was the group of members dating back to the late 1980s or early 1990s, judged to be the least naturally aligned with Polanski, being instinctively suspicious of anything which looked like a conventional twentieth-century leftwing project, and indeed possibly outrightly conservative in their politics.

It was hypothesised that a winning coalition could be built across these wings of the party, especially if the campaign could inspire the first camp to swell with a few thousand further members before the deadline for new joiners to have voting rights in the leadership election. In the end, the strength of support for Polanski's platform among the membership shocked even his closest allies. One of the most poignant examples of Polanski's ability to win support from all parts of the party was referenced in his victory speech: a woman had got in touch with Polanski to tell him she had joined a political party – the Greens – for the first time in her life, having been inspired by his campaign. Moreover, her mother had *re-joined* the party, after having been a lapsed member of what was then known as the Ecology Party many decades ago. Here in microcosm was a bridge between the most recent converts and the oldest stalwarts of the Green movement.

Polanski's relative lack of name recognition among the public worked to his advantage in the early going of the race, his campaign adding intrigue and a sense of fresh blood to an election which the media class probably thought would be completely without competition. Generally speaking, Green Party leadership elections pass without much mention beyond perfunctory acknowledgement in the *Guardian*. On this occasion, the exposure surpassed anything the Green Party had experienced in its history of internal elections, bolstered by an establishment media thrilled to have a figure to occupy vacated space in the political landscape to Starmer's expansive left, along with a grassroots leftwing media more sincerely (if cautiously) pleased to have a figure who seemed capable of advancing their political interests.

On the day that he launched the campaign in the *Guardian*, Polanski also appeared on Politics Joe and Novara Live, and was booked for slots by Times Radio, the *New Statesman* and Channel 4. He barely stopped for breath thereafter. Polanski would later reveal that the party had more Google searches in two weeks than it had had in 20 years. All of this was evidence of the good planning Polanski had put into his bid, amassing an organised team in the weeks leading up to the launch, ensuring everything was in place from top-line strategy to the nuts and bolts of scripts for social media content. It also meant that his campaign manager Ruthra-Rajan could barely get hold of him. "We were a victim of our own success," she remembers. "We weren't quite expecting there to be quite that much media that early on and that consistently." All of this seemed to catch incumbent rival Ramsay unawares, whose campaign throughout gave the impression of someone unprepared and in full expectation of being effectively unchallenged. Through the exposure earned from this well coordinated splash, Polanski's gifts as a national class political communicator became abundantly clear to the media, the public and – most crucially – the membership of the Green Party. This was achieved through a combination of four key factors: personal charisma, compelling messaging, tight discipline and an ability to deploy all of this across both traditional broadcast media and newer digital platforms.

Polanski's communications style was unapologetically populist and met the public where they were at by foregrounding the cost-of-living crisis, which perpetually topped polls as the number one issue that concerned the electorate. This was enhanced by a degree of message discipline which had hitherto eluded Green spokespeople: using every single media opportunity given to him to unify the 99 per cent against the vanishingly small capitalist elite who were driving unprecedented levels of inequality in the country. Daily he advocated for a wealth tax. This had a threefold advantage: it responded to the material concerns of a majority of the public; it signalled to the Left a willingness to engage in the politics of class antagonism; and it furthermore appealed to median Green members in its systemic analysis of how wealth inequality drives environmental degradation as well as social disaster.

Back when the question of whether a new party of the Left ought to be founded was a live and contested issue, many of the commentators involved in the debate advocated for a communications approach carrying a striking resemblance to what Polanski was putting into practice through this sort of advocacy for a wealth tax. This is Labour's former director of communications James Schneider, writing in the pamphlet *Your Party*, in favour of the formation of a new Left party which had the ability to build majoritarian appeal:

> We should reject all the pieties of the political media state class, for they are hated by the public and rightly so. We should create controversies rather than retreating from them. This communicative style is often called left-populism. It involves drawing a big, bold line of antagonism in which there is unity on our side and division on the other. That line of antagonism is extremely simple: the reason for our problems is the bankers and the billionaires. They are at war with us, so we are going to war with them. We should aim to baffle and outrage the media establishment with a political style that is combative but also joyful.[53]

Here Schneider speaks directly to the schism on the Left which would define the contortions into which the founders of Your Party would twist themselves. Should a political project situated to the left of Labour have mass and majoritarian appeal, acting pluralistically to unite socialists, social democrats and others of broadly aligned values and political goals? Or ought it to be uncompromisingly purist in its anti-capitalist and socialist ideology, despite the limitations that might put on its immediate-term public support? In principle, mass appeal and ideological commitment are not by definition mutually exclusive. In practice, the best approximation of the former came in the form of Polanski's leadership pitch, while the likes of the nascent leadership of Your Party defined themselves by an increasingly inflexible commitment to the latter.

The best example of Polanski's populism with mass appeal came in the form of an arresting video posted on social media in late July, shot cinematically on the shore next to the cliffs of Dover. Polanski spoke to camera about meeting a man who wished he had a gun so that he could shoot people arriving in small boats. Compellingly and emotively, the script invited the viewer to turn their fury from some of the most desperate people on earth being deliberately scapegoated and towards the billionaires hoarding wealth, assets and opportunity. Written and directed by Jeremy Clancy – responsible for some of the best content put out by Corbyn during his time as Labour leader – it reached over a million people by the time Polanski was live on primetime LBC the following evening. Content posted by Ramsay on the same day reached about 400 people in the same period of time. Polanski's video went on to reach over 3 million people, all told.

Clancy would continue to work with Polanski once he was elected leader, to perhaps even greater effect on a pair of political party broadcasts, widely lauded as some of the best political communications in many years, earning effusive praise from figures as unlikely as Alistair Campbell.[54] In one, he walks the streets of Leeds as daybreak creeps into the sky, nostalgic for days of "ordinary hope" when people could reasonably aspire for an improving standard of living, rather than the spiralling decline in which we find ourselves. Crucially, he again names our enemy: the people who make more money while they sleep than most people earn in a lifetime of work. Another equally brilliant video saw Polanski running the streets, literally breathlessly listing the piling economic pressures, humiliations and disappointments of modern life for a growing number of people. "What if the answer," he asks the viewer, "isn't to keep running? What if the most powerful thing we can do – all of us, all together at once – is to stop running?" Then, he suggests, we would see that while most of us are running faster and faster to create wealth, it's not coming back to our communities – it's being sucked upwards.

In a political landscape where party broadcasts have had almost no relevance as a means of mass communication for at least a decade, these films crossed over into organic virality across social media platforms, reaching millions. During his leadership campaign, Polanski established a social media strategy which would continue to reap rewards as leader: sharing attacks from the billionaire-owned press as evidence of the power Greens were building, and encouraging more people to join the movement. The lines of antagonism were clearly drawn. So, too, were the positive visions for a fairer society on a safer planet.

While Polanski's leadership campaign was cutting through, evidence piled up that his opponents had failed to do the same. During the head-to-head debate between Polanski and Ramsay on the *Today* programme towards the close of the contest, presenter Nick Robinson audibly faltered as he tried – and failed – to recall Chowns' name, settling instead for referring to her, cringe-inducingly, as "another candidate".

Polling throughout was particularly unkind to Ramsay. In late July 2025, YouGov reported higher favourability ratings for Polanski than Ramsay or Chowns among 2024 Green voters.[55] Most damningly, in August, YouGov reported the startling fact that 87 per cent *of people who voted Green in 2024* didn't know who Ramsay was when shown a photograph of him. Only 9 per cent could identify him correctly. To put this in some context: Farage was recognised by 98 per cent of his voters.[56] For all the merits and qualities Ramsay possesses, this was clearly a completely unconscionable situation for a party leader seeking re-election. By contrast, by May 2026, polling revealed that over a quarter of the British public at large recognised Zack Polanski.[57]

As the campaign progressed, it became more and more apparent that the momentum and the membership were tipping towards Polanski, with the Ramsay and Chowns campaign actively alienating members. A notable example was a social media post which proclaimed, "We're not here to hold signs, we're here to hold power," clearly intended as a malign comment on Polanski's promise to build a wider social movement and base for progressive change outside of Parliament. This had the effect of annoying even members who might naturally be warmly disposed towards Ramsay and Chowns, widely perceived as being disrespectful to the many thousands of Green activists who have dutifully posed behind candidates (including Ramsay and Chowns) holding "Vote Green" signs. Of course, Ramsay and Chowns were also inevitably taunted with pictures of themselves holding signs in aid of various campaigns over the years. Most substantively, this betrayed the campaign's apparent belief that winning seats in Parliament was the totality of the Green Party's ambitions, whereas the median member of the party would proudly believe and recognise that it holds at least some role in wider movement building, campaigning and cultural change.

It didn't take long for the central pitch they were making to members to crumble. You could take on its own terms the claim that parliamentarians were inherently more suitable spokespeople for the party, that Polanski's platform was inherently alienating to a coalition of voters required to make electoral advances, and that Ramsay and Chowns were better placed to lead the party to the next level of success. It's a coherent hypothesis. But it did not survive contact with reality through the course of the campaign, with the ceiling of Polanski's support – both in the membership and the country – clearly demonstrated to be higher than Ramsay and Chowns', evidenced everywhere from anecdote to hard polling.

Never was this more on display than the raft of hustings which took place over the summer, a few of which were on national platforms such as the *New Statesman*'s podcast and live LBC radio. Both were combative, but the latter provided one of the campaign's most notorious moments when Ramsay point blank refused to answer the question of whether he "liked" Polanski, to the utter astonishment of moderator and presenter Iain Dale.

For a candidate whose supposed strength was premised on his ability to deliver safe, professionalised political communications that was able to build mass appeal among moderates, this failure to show basic deference to his sitting deputy was a baffling spectacle. "They just seem to take any media opportunity they had to slag off Zack," remembers Ruthra-Rajan, "and all it did was work for us." In this sense, the campaign run by Ramsay and Chowns was a small-scale parallel to the unwittingly helpful attacks that would follow from the billionaire press. By contrast, Polanski's ability to think on his feet and communicate clearly was apparent. At a final hustings in London before voting opened to members, the *Guardian*'s Andrew Sparrow gave a snap verdict, saying that Polanski was in a "different league" to Chowns.[58]

By the closing weeks, the Ramsay and Chowns campaign was limping to the finish line with examples of casual incompetency, like tweeting that there were seven days left to vote when there were actually five (a post which stayed published), blended with a growing sense of panic from their team and their outriders. Most memorably, about a fortnight from polls closing, an anonymous source close to Ramsay and Chowns was reported to have said that the thousands of new members attracted to Polanski's campaign felt like a "hostile takeover" of the party.[59] In the very same *Guardian* article, Polanski's colleague on the London Assembly Caroline Russell came out in support of his leadership after having stayed neutral through the campaign until that point. You would struggle to find a figure more beloved by all wings of the party, or more unlikely to be associated with any form of hostility, least of all one which undermined her own party.

The most credible threat to Polanski's campaign didn't come from his opponents but from outside the Green Party. Days after voting opened for the Green Party leadership election, Zarah Sultana – the leftwing MP elected as a Labour candidate but stripped of the whip for voting against the two-child benefit cap – posted on social media to say that she would be co-founding a new leftwing party with Jeremy Corbyn. Almost immediately, however, came the first evidence of the well-documented rank incompetence and conflict which has plagued the project for its duration – rumours quickly circulating that Corbyn had not authorised the announcement. This kicked into motion a spiral of events which are still unravelling to this day.

Nevertheless, Sultana's portal attracted 800,000 email sign-ups, and polling suggested that such a vehicle could attract 15 per cent of the vote. This polling of a hypothetical proposition inevitably resulted in different interpretations from different people, depending on what they wanted it to reveal. For Ramsay and Chowns' campaign, it was evidence that Polanski's opportunistic pitch for political space was dead on arrival. The media class followed suit, acting as if the new party already existed, resulting in the bewildering spectacle of an establishment media which a decade ago tried to crush Corbynism now trying to will it into being. Routinely it was reported by people who should know better that Corbyn and Sultana's new party (there was no party) had 800,000 members (it did not). For some hard-left activists, the polling was evidence of a latent desire within the public for a myriad of things, ranging from radical experiments in participatory democracy to a loose federation of existing independent candidates and groupings.

The one thing you could confidently say that the polling actually showed was that there was a good chunk of the British electorate that still supported something similar to the 2017 Labour manifesto and that they would like to see some frontline politicians advocating for those sorts of reforms. This was the fundamental political reality which powered Polanski's campaign. With voting open, there was high confidence that the momentum within the membership had put Polanski firmly out front. Whether he would find himself in political space when it was time to face the country was for the time being an open question.

It is, of course, easier to feel the confidence of victory in retrospect. As voting closed, until the day of the result, there was a background hum of doubt in the campaign team that, while Polanski had clearly dominated the media war, there was every possibility that Ramsay and Chowns' campaign had been running a more sophisticated and effective peer-to-peer canvassing operation among actual party members. Furthermore, episodes like getting sidelined into a rabbit hole about NATO early in the campaign and garnering the support of notable figures closely associated with Corbynism, such as economists James Meadway (who backed Polanski in a *New Statesman* op-ed) and Grace Blakeley (who came out as a newly joined Green live on LBC), caused some of the team to worry that it had focussed on attracting the disillusioned Left at the expense of reaching the established, actually existing Green membership – or, worse still, actively inflating an anti-Zack turnout among more conservative members. "I did a 180 on whether it's a good idea to actively try to recruit new members to vote in internal elections," Ruthra-Rajan admits:

> Just because it massively complicates who you're trying to talk to the whole time. I was worried about certain groups and certain people like a lot of the older Green Party members, and a lot of the ones that would be swayed by Caroline Lucas. I did even hear from a couple of the councillors directly as well, just saying: I love Zack, but can you just ask him to remember rural constituencies? That was why I was always trying to get him to remember that it's not just about all the new members coming in.

Still, there were strong grounds for believing that Polanski had reached beyond his natural base in the membership and had won over a winning coalition of Greens – from the 100 councillors across the country who endorsed Polanski to the many well-reputed campaign managers who backed him too, including the campaign manager who oversaw Ramsay's outgoing co-leader's election to Bristol Central. Indicators like these suggested that the claims that Polanski was neither able to appeal to rural areas nor someone who takes winning elections seriously were not resonating with the active membership. The day before the result, Find Out Now had Polanski winning with 65 per cent.[60] In the end, Polanski swept the membership with an unprecedented mandate of 85 per cent, and one of the highest turnouts in party history. For all the accusations of entryism, and the real upsurge in membership which was the result of a campaign which had inspired politically homeless people on the Left, even if the reported 8 per cent increase of membership across June had all voted for Ramsay and Chowns, Polanski still would have walked it.[61]

Few people saw the scale of this victory coming. But when you take a step back and consider the role the leader of the Green Party of England and Wales actually occupies, it becomes less surprising. The leadership election was commonly framed as a decisive battle over two competing future directions for the party, and no doubt the candidates had starkly different visions for political communications and strategy. That said, the democratic structure of the party places pretty hard limits on the power the leader of the Green Party actually wields and does not provide a strong parallel with leadership positions in other parties. The leader of the Greens cannot set policy. Indeed, any member who joined to vote for Polanski would have exactly the same voting rights as him at the next party conference. Members set policy and the leaders are constitutionally duty bound to go out and advocate for it. And in that narrow sense, for all the ways in which this race was framed as some sort of referendum on fundamental political strategy, the leadership is in a very real sense primarily a spokesperson role.

From that perspective, it's pretty obvious why Polanski's qualities carried him to victory. One thing which unites all wings and tendencies of the party, and which frequently can be relied upon to mobilise the membership, is the deep-rooted belief that the Greens are being denied – or are denying themselves – a requisite platform in the national conversation. For over a decade, Greens have watched in dismay at the way in which Farage has been able to make the political weather. With that traction now translating into surging polling and real-life election results through the vehicle of Reform, this nagging sense of injustice evolved into justified dread. In Polanski, members of all backgrounds were offered what they longed for: someone who had the capacity to cut through in the digital and broadcast landscape with uncompromised advocacy of Green policy.

"People were desperate for something real and policies that are about compassion and just the practicalities of being able to get by day to day," Ruthra-Rajan says, "but no one else is really talking about that. He does the work, so he is prepped. He is able to respond to things. And he does genuinely try to answer every question. I think it's so rare."

That's how, on 2 September 2025, Zack Polanski was ushered into a packed room on London's Coin Street in front of an unprecedented array of the country's mainstream print and broadcast media to be announced as the new leader of the Green Party of England and Wales. This stood in stark contrast to previous election result announcements, typically conducted in a tiny, unceremonious room with maybe one *Guardian* journalist and a few bloggers. This was an event. His speech encapsulated the eco-populist programme which would define his leadership, grounding political failure and environmental destruction in people's material concerns:

> People in this country are exhausted. They are tired. They are sick of working long hours and never feeling secure. They see water companies pump sewage into our waters and charge us extra for the privilege. And they see how broken the old two-party system is. We know this political space has been ripe for charlatans like Nigel Farage and Reform. Millionaires who are pretending to serve working-class communities but who are actually backed by the same billionaires who are

> destroying our democracies, our communities and our planet. So it is an absolute moral responsibility at this moment for the Green Party to step up with the bold politics that I know we have. To say to people that we can, and we will, lower your bills. We will nationalise the water companies. We will hold this Labour government to account. Because when we look at Keir Starmer and what this government have been doing, whether it's the two-child benefit cap, the disability cuts, the genocide in Gaza, my message to Labour is very clear: we are not here to be disappointed by you. We are not here to be concerned by you. We are here to replace you.[62]

The most high-profile and competitive leadership election in party history had culminated in its most emphatically decisive result. Members were not cowed by the endorsements – and warnings – of the party establishment figures who backed the cautious and notionally more professionalised campaign of the incumbent parliamentarians. The membership instead overwhelmingly backed a proudly ecosocialist, openly insurgent candidate with his sights on turning the Green Party into the primary, mass electoral project of the Left in the UK. Here was a united Green Party, ready to build majoritarian support for radical politics. Here, too, was a Green Party which was still proudly rooted in its own past. Because Polanski wasn't a rupture with the party's history. He was the natural culmination of the principled progress the party had made during its existence, particularly within the last decade-and-a-half of Conservative rule. The seeds of Zack Polanski's leadership were planted during the long 2010s.

3

The Long 2010s

During the 2015 general election campaign, the then Green Party leader Natalie Bennett debated a future prime minister. Not David Cameron, who was already prime minister. Nor was it any of the other party leaders in the seven-way debate broadcast to around 7 million people on ITV, none of whom have made it to the top of the mountain at the moment of writing – although time will tell with regard to Farage (then UKIP leader) or, indeed, as an outside bet, Ed Miliband. Away from the glare of the television studio lights, Natalie Bennett encountered at least one future prime minister at a hustings for the parliamentarian seat she was contesting, where the local Labour candidate was Sir Keir Starmer.

Comfortably holding the Holborn and St Pancras seat for Labour in succession to the outgoing MP Frank Dobson, this was the election in which Starmer took his place in Parliament, before climbing through Corbyn's shadow cabinet (the very idea of a "Corbyn's shadow cabinet" still *completely* unthinkable in May 2015), becoming leader in 2020 on the basis of quickly abandoned pledges, and eventually prime minister in 2024. For anyone in the audience that night, it would have been impossible to imagine where the next ten years would take Keir Starmer. But there was another person on stage for whom the same could be said. The Liberal Democrat representative, who wasn't even the local candidate, and extremely inexperienced by his own admission, would likely not warrant mentioning in 2026 were it not for the path his politics took after meeting Natalie Bennett that evening. His name was Zack Polanski.

"I remember Keir Starmer going really hard on Natalie," Polanski recalls over a decade later.

> He'd say: "It's so easy for the Greens because whatever Labour announces, they just announce they'll double it, triple it, but they've got no way to pay for it." And I remember Natalie being so strong in terms of talking about investment, and in terms of talking about the fact that the Labour opposition at that point didn't have a plan to reverse austerity. I remember being struck by how seriously she took the issues and her commitment.

Polanski and Bennett subsequently ended up on several Make Votes Matter panels together, as part of their advocacy for electoral reform. "The thing I remember more than anything," Polanski admits "was coming home and speaking to my partner and just saying: 'She's right! She's just right about a lot of things.' And I've got these lines to say, but ultimately I think her arguments are more compelling."

That fateful night in St Pancras is just one particularly striking moment in the story of how the threads of Zack Polanski's eventual leadership started being woven throughout the preceding decade. The 2010–24 period of British Conservative rule corresponded with a period of a step change in prominence for the Greens, as well as being their period of fastest maturation – until being eclipsed by the current surge under Polanski. It began with the party winning its first ever parliamentary representation, on the same night David Cameron won enough seats to make him prime minister, and culminated in the Greens doing what had eluded them in three subsequent general elections, and what many feared was effectively impossible under first past the post: returning more than one MP. On the night the Conservatives were eviscerated in 2024, the Greens quadrupled their seats in the Commons.

In those intervening years, their membership had grown by tens of thousands (with some notable fluctuations, discussed later in this chapter) and they'd gone from around 100 councillors to over 800 across the country.[63] A landmark moment in popular support came when it most decisively outflanked Labour to its left in the early years of austerity under the coalition government, with over a million people voting for their principled programme of anti-austerity in the 2015 general election.[64] This chapter tells the story of how the Greens played their part in creating some of these conditions, opening up space for opportunities for the Left and, ultimately, Polanski's own election to leader. It looks at the limitations they hit and some of the lessons the party can learn going forward. It's a period of some striking parallels with Polanski's leadership today: insurgency, populism, surging growth, and support won through principled positions. It began in Brighton on 6 May 2010.

Anyone vaguely left of centre who stayed up all night to watch the 2010 general election results roll in will have spent most of their time biting their nails wondering if a Labour–Liberal Democrat coalition might be a viable outcome by dawn as a front-running Conservative Party pulled closer and closer to a majority. But a welcome ray of light came in the early morning when the then Green Party leader Caroline Lucas was elected to Parliament to represent Brighton Pavilion as the first ever MP for the Green Party of England and Wales. Stepping forward to the lectern amid noisy celebration from her local party members and campaign team, she thanked Brighton for making history, and for "putting the politics of hope above the politics of fear".[65] Sadly, such hope was about to collide headfirst into the hard reality of a Conservative austerity agenda. Following an election campaign which had focussed on the supposed need to cut the deficit, the Cameron–Clegg coalition government got on with the job of balancing the books on the backs of the poorest and most vulnerable. In his June Budget, Chancellor George Osborne announced the deepest ever cuts to the public sector.[66]

Betrayal can unleash potent reactions. On the streets, across the country, a resurgent and angry wave of leftwing activism was exploding into life. Students were enraged by the lies told to them by Liberal Democrat politicians who – to a person – had signed a pledge to scrap tuition fees during the general election campaign only for about half of them to support tripling fees within months of forming a coalition government. This was met with a ferocious militancy that Britain hadn't seen since the poll tax riots, beginning with a demonstration which famously saw the Conservative Party headquarters trashed, and culminating in a night of rioting and police brutality following the vote which condemned a generation to a working life of debt. Caroline Lucas, for her part, addressed the protesters outside Parliament and voted against the measures. Incidentally, this left the Greens as the only party in England committed to upholding the same free education that had benefitted many of the MPs who had just voted to further deny it to the ascending generation. Greens remain a lonely voice within frontline politics advocating for this today.

The force and the tenacity of this explosion of student activism stimulated further resistance to the full programme of austerity which emanated from the Cameron–Clegg premiership, as chronicled by one of the organisers of the student protests, Michael Chessum, in his book *This Is Only the Beginning*.[67] Groups like UK Uncut and Disabled People Against the Cuts made a massive contribution to the fight against the decimation of our public services and welfare state, and such various strands were eventually brought together under the banner of the People's Assembly Against Austerity. This evidenced a widespread constituency in the country of people who were deeply opposed to savage cuts to the public realm and understood that opposition to be rooted in their own material interest. Relative to the tens of thousands regularly flooding the streets, the Greens were by definition a marginal presence in this movement at the outset of the decade. But as the years wore on, and as the financial cuts were increasingly felt, a growing number of these people (and their allies in wider society) would seek more formal political representation away from the horizontalist, quasi-anarchist direct-action movement. Labour was not offering it. The Greens would.

In 2012, Caroline Lucas announced that she would not be re-standing as a leadership candidate, saying that she wanted to make room for more figures to rise through the party. Her successor Natalie Bennett was a former *Guardian* journalist, and member of the party's elected executive. Like Polanski today, Bennett took full advantage of not being shackled to Westminster, instead turning her attention to two key objectives: raising the profile of the Greens in the media and helping swell the membership and capacity of local parties. If Natalie had kept all the train tickets she must have racked up from 2012 to 2015, she would have quite an impressive display – hitting the rails with an indefatigable willingness to address almost any meeting of Greens and allies, no matter how remote the location or desolate the attendance numbers. The graft paid off. By the end of Bennett's first two-year term as leader, membership had doubled. Then, during the remarkable wave of support enjoyed as part of the 2015 general election campaign, membership swelled to a high point of 68,500 in what came to be known (albeit now dwarfed by comparison with Polanski's membership explosion) as the Green surge.

Bennett's leadership contained within it various precursors to Polanski's. The first was a defiantly leftwing communications strategy which shrewdly occupied the vast open space vacated by Labour, who could not bring themselves to oppose the punitive economic shock therapy and social cruelty unleashed by the Tories. Ed Miliband would make a habit of addressing anti-austerity rallies by meekly complaining that the wrong type of cuts were being made, rather than actually opposing them. His shadow chancellor Ed Balls said in a 2012 interview with the *Guardian* that "we are going to have to keep all these cuts" and backed George Osborne's public sector pay freeze.[68] When this was the primary electoral alternative, millions were left politically homeless. Bennett stepped into this space with confidence, proudly articulating the party's anti-austerity stance, backing the public sector and welfare state from BBC's Broadcasting House to village hall meetings.

The second parallel with Polanski was Bennett's determination to transcend the pigeonholing of the Greens as a pressure group with a narrow interest in rigidly defined environmental matters. As we will see in Chapter 4, the Greens have always had encoded into their political analysis and aspirations a sense of the intersections between social, economic and environmental justice, but it would take decades of battling upstream against its own stereotypes to convince the media and the electorate that Greens were anything more than friendly gardeners. Natalie's use of anti-austerity politics broadened her platform, allowing her to articulate a more holistic political offer on a national stage for the first time in the party's history.

"For the first couple of years," Natalie tells me, thinking back, "every time I'd be on telly there'd either be a wind turbine or a rubbish dump behind me". But in 2014, Natalie achieved a watershed moment for the party: appearing on Radio 4's *Westminster Hour* to debate welfare reform.[69] This was the first time that she had been invited onto the mainstream media to talk about a core bread-and-butter economics issue without any ostensible connection to environmental policy. "The media had *just* started to notice," she remembers, "that we were about more than whales and trees." Another notable example came in the form of a speech given in the Romanian Cultural Institute, covered by the BBC, warning that the escalating rhetoric around immigration was at risk of inflaming tensions in the public, with the potential to spill into violence.[70] Along with opposition to anti-austerity, this defence and celebration of migrants became another cornerstone of the Greens' values-based offer to the electorate, for which millions were grateful, owing to the failure of all the major parties to show any compassion or principle on the matter.

The third parallel with today: Bennett's tenure saw the party's first foray into a form of insurgent, populist communications which would, if sporadically, continue to characterise the party's tone of voice thereafter. Lacking the overt class antagonism which would provide the basis of Polanski's political positioning in the present day, the party nonetheless used arch irony and humour to lampoon a despised political establishment, adding a string to the bow of the earnest communications style so effectively hitherto employed by Lucas. The most celebrated example of this was the party election broadcast of 2015. Beginning with a typical, dry monologue to camera, it panned to a full-scale music video production of dry smoke and glittering Union Jacks: four men in blue, yellow, red and purple (UKIP) ties singing in literal harmony, unified in their commitment to austerity. This racked up over a million views on YouTube alone, marking the party's first experiences of online virality. [71]

Where Polanski has built on these foundations is obvious. He is, by Bennett's own admission, a more effective communicator than she was. There were, of course, notorious examples of this from Bennett's time in post, not least the fairly disastrous day upon which she launched the 2015 general election campaign when time stood still as she shuffled papers in silence, getting numbers wrong while complaining of a cold, live on LBC with a gleeful Nick Ferrari.[72] These moments of disaster did not evidence a uniquely incapable media performer but instead pointed more broadly to the fact that the Greens were in a state of infrastructural infancy and struggling to survive contact with the realities of a newly established 24-hour news cycle of live broadcast. Put simply, Bennett did not have the staff support a party leader required. Perhaps the best example of this was Bennett cheerfully turning up to BBC Broadcasting House believing herself to be participating in a fairly routine panel discussion for a few minutes on *Sunday Politics*, only to discover – moments before going live on air – that she had been booked for a 20-minute one-on-one grilling with Andrew Neil. It should have been impossible for a major party leader to have been put in that position.

Limitations and missteps aside, these key ingredients of providing a principled leftwing offer which transcended narrow environmental interests and delivered with a twist of insurgency clearly laid down the blueprint of Polanski's success today. Added together, they had, in their own modest way for its time, a similar effect to Polanski's leadership: an explosion in formal support in terms of both membership and votes. With the added exposure of the broadcasting rules around the general election, coupled with a fairly dismal campaign from Miliband's Labour, the Greens chalked up over a million votes in 2015, nearly quadrupling their total relative to 2010, and ascended to over 68,000 members – surpassing both UKIP and the Liberal Democrats.[73] Owing to the distortions of first past the post, this step change in popular support did not return any new Greens to Parliament. But it did give political expression to a significant and growing constituency of people across the country who opposed austerity and wanted a more radical policy programme than what the narrowly concentrated neoliberal political establishment was dishing up.

Of all the people disgusted by Labour's capitulation to the Conservatives' austerity and anti-migrant agenda, few were more dismayed than Labour members themselves. They would reassert themselves by electing Jeremy Corbyn, a backbencher socialist barely known to the wider public, as leader of the Labour Party in the late summer of 2015. The Blairite candidate Liz Kendall was knocked into a distant fourth out of four as the widespread support for Corbyn, and the politics to which he was giving voice, became palpable throughout the summer's extraordinary campaign. A great deal was made of the change to the voting system which meant that so-called "supporters" paying a £3 fee could vote in the Labour leadership election, providing a low bar of entry for the swelling social movements which had either supported the Greens in 2015 or inchoately opposed austerity on the streets. These rule changes had, ironically, been supported by the right of the party, in the belief that it would diminish the influence of trade union voting blocs and introduce a moderating effect from the wider public. This theory did not take into account the possibility that the centre of political gravity in the country, particularly on economic issues, might swing far to the left of the Blairite consensus.

That said, while the Labour establishment cried foul over accusations of "entryism" (the attempt of small, organised, non-representative groups to capture a larger political body), this complaint did not survive contact with political reality. The Parliamentary Labour Party had ended up far to the right of its own membership and, indeed, by many measures, the wider public. While Blairites told scare stories about Trotskyite takeovers (the official membership of such groups probably totalling in the low thousands in 2015), accusations swirled over party officials scouring these £3 supporters to find any justification for throwing them out.[74] All of this was ultimately wasted effort. The fact was that even without the £3 voters, Corbyn would still have walked it.[75] In this we find an echo in Polanski's leadership election ten years later, with his internal opponents decrying the "hostile takeover" of what they viewed as the washed-up survivors of Corbynism flooding into the party to remake it in their own image. As with Corbyn in the preceding decade, these numbers were ultimately negligible in the face of the overwhelming mandate he received from the pre-existing membership.

The effect that Corbyn's election had on the Green surge of 2015 was to send its wave crashing into the rocks. Of the tens of thousands of people who had swelled the Greens' membership in 2015, many jumped ship to Labour in order to support an anti-austerity platform which was being articulated by the official opposition, rather than a fringe party which was hovering in single-digit percentage polling. At the 2017 snap election, Greens could do little but watch as the party's vote share more than halved relative to the million plus it achieved just two years earlier.[76]

Few people feel comfortable saying so, but the Greens had helped set the conditions for Corbynism, and this is evidenced in the way that Corbynism can be seen as a wholly coherent continuation of what the Greens were offering in the 2015 general election. While the rightwing press fell over themselves to smear Corbyn as an unreformed communist, and the organised Left of the country projected their own hopes onto the first major figure in modern political history who was broadly aligned to their goals, the actually existing political offer of Corbynism was sometimes obscured – and it bore striking resemblance to the Greens under Natalie Bennett, both in content and presentation. The professor of political and cultural theory Jeremy Gilbert captured something of this in his observation that Corbynism offered a moral critique of austerity, not a political critique of neoliberalism.[77] In this he made implicit criticism of Corbyn relative to a figure like Bernie Sanders, who spoke more convincingly and explicitly in terms of class antagonism. What he didn't draw attention to, however, is how he had also perfectly described the Greens' communications and political strategy for the first half of the decade. The platform the Greens had earned during the 2015 general election helped widen the political horizon during a contest in which the economic consensus around the necessity of delivering austerity would otherwise have gone completely unchallenged. Having Bennett at podiums next to Miliband on national television exposed the cowardice of his position.

Corbyn as a communicator was similar to Lucas and Bennett in terms of the content of his critique. Corbynism as a political project was the sort of social democratic reform which, while a notable break from the British Thatcherite consensus of the preceding decades, was basically a typical centre-left platform in most other normal European countries. Put simply, as a political offer, the 2017 Labour manifesto was very similar to the 2015 Green Party manifesto. Needless to say, Corbyn as a figure more naturally appealed to certain political tendencies owing to his long-standing association with formal Left traditions in a way which no figure from the Greens could then realistically emulate. As an actual political project, though, the most obvious – and perhaps only – distinguishing feature was that Labour was a vehicle through which you could plausibly win state power and form a government. For understandable reasons, this was a more instinctively attractive offer for thousands of activists and millions of voters.

Given all of this, it is difficult to imagine what the Greens could have done to arrest the collapse of the support they had quickly amassed during the 2015 general election campaign. Nor can one easily imagine what Bennett or an alternative leader could have done from 2010 to 2015 to build that support in a way which was resilient to the Labour Party adopting a communications strategy offering a direct critique of austerity and a political programme of social democratic reform which represented a decisive break from neoliberal consensus. Like Polanski today, Bennett had moved into open political space, without compromising on political substance. The Greens had not simply conjured up an opportunistic anti-austerity platform which became redundant upon the election of Corbyn. The policy platform predated the political opportunity. What Bennett did so successfully was to use the political moment to transcend the pigeonholes and stereotypes of the Greens and communicate the party's wider policy offer to millions more people. But when a more viable electoral project moved into that political space, the Greens were displaced. The obvious question today, of course: is Polanski's surge vulnerable to the same risk?

The second half of the 2010s saw the party rebuild some support following the rollercoaster of the Green surge and the Corbyn crash. The primary basis of this reconstitution happened to be one of the harbingers of Corbynism's own demise: the 2016 vote to leave the European Union. Again, the Greens occupied clear political space which had been ceded by Labour, and they did so in complete consistency with long-held and long-advocated positions. In this case: a radical case for Remain, speaking to a huge constituency of the country which had been abandoned by a subtler manifestation of Labour capitulation to the parties on its right. (In pledging to abandon freedom of movement, for example, Labour went into the 2017 general election with a policy on migration which was arguably to the right of that which they put to the country in 2015.) The electoral rewards for the Greens were evidenced by the extraordinary European elections of 2019, in which the Labour and Conservative votes collapsed, and the Greens raced ahead – picking up four new MEPs (including the future leadership contender Ellie Chowns). The Greens were also aided by an unprecedented surge in the salience of climate politics. Street movements like Extinction Rebellion and School Strikes for Climate, along with record-breaking temperatures and climate impacts in the UK, rocketed climate and nature into the top three concerns of the British public by the end of 2019.

While this combination of Remain and climate provided the Greens something of an electoral niche relative to their nadir of utter marginalisation in the 2017 general election, they were ultimately unable to find and occupy the sort of political space which Bennett enjoyed in the first half of 2010, let alone that which Polanski filled in 2025. This ability to find space is pivotal to success. Polanski's qualities as a leader and communicator have only been able to actualise the Greens' current fortunes when combined with political opportunity. Other Green figures from the second half of the 2010s, who could be seen as partial precursors to Polanski, could not revitalise the prospects of the Greens without such a gap in the political landscape.

One such figure was Jonathan Bartley, elected as a co-leader of the party alongside Caroline Lucas in 2016, and who was a more fluently combative communicator than the party had hitherto produced. His first episode of political prominence came when he directly confronted David Cameron regarding the Conservatives' policies on special educational needs, happening to bump into him while taking his disabled son to a hospital appointment during the 2015 general election campaign, all gratefully captured by TV news cameras. His subsequent leadership of the Greens was characterised by this confidence to directly confront powerful political actors from Iain Duncan Smith to bosses in the fracking industry. Sharing one of Polanski's foremost qualities, he was hungry to pick political fights to draw useful lines of division and confer attention upon the party's principled positions.

A second, very distinct figure came in the form of Magid Magid, a Somali British Sheffield councillor who had spent time in a refugee camp as a child before becoming Lord Mayor of

Sheffield at the age of 28, and whose breathtaking official portrait of him squatting on a pillar of his City Hall went completely viral. A subsequent photograph of Magid wearing a shirt with the slogan "Donald Trump Is a Wasteman" stimulated a similarly electric online response and inspired countless copycat uses of the slogan on protests of Trump's subsequent visits to the UK. But with the broad Left's hopes still understandably hitched to a last ditch effort to get Corbynism over the line, however, neither figure found themselves in the political conditions to fully reconstitute nor extend a meaningful surge of support for the Greens despite some potential ability, in different ways, to command the same sort of appeal that Polanski does today. It would take the collapse of both the main parties from 2023 onwards to open the sort of space the Greens had once found under Natalie Bennett.

When Polanski won the leadership, his victory speech contained a pledge to replace Labour. Ten years prior, this would have been laughable. Even comparatively modest pledges like running in 75 per cent of seats and winning ten new MPs were considered (rightly, as it turned out) to be pie in the sky in 2015. Today, while still undoubtedly a bold aspiration, the prospect of the Greens supplanting Labour as the primary political party of the Left is not something anyone can dismiss out of hand, just as it seems extremely possible that Reform has supplanted the Conservatives. Only the 2029 general election will confirm this for sure, but all the available evidence points towards a genuine and long-term reconstitution of the British electoral landscape being underway, contrary to the more transient surges of support for smaller parties seen in the mid-2010s. This opens up the possibility of the Greens successfully consolidating their position today in a way which would have been impossible ten years ago.

The two routes for Labour to successfully displace the Greens today would be either for its Left to recapture the leadership and regain the support which has decamped to the Greens, or for the party to otherwise rebuild its historical voting bloc of 30–40 per cent from anywhere within the electorate. Neither of these things seem likely. Under Starmer's leadership, a frenzied project has been undertaken to ensure that nobody from the Left comes within sight of the leadership ever again, primarily through a process of hand-selecting MPs to gerrymander the composition of the Parliamentary Labour Party. Having liked a tweet by Caroline Lucas was enough to get you blocked from standing.[78] There are never total impossibilities in politics, but the prospects of another Corbyn wresting the leadership of Labour are negligible.

The other route – reassembling a winning coalition of voters from anywhere in the electorate – is more plausible, but still remote. The results of attempting to appease parties on its right while trying to retain the voters on its left (by sneering at them, curiously) are now plain for all to see: a freefall collapse in the polls and the most unpopular prime minister ever, hitting the sorts of numbers from which there are no obvious historical precedents of recovery. A Burnham-led Labour presents the most obvious danger to the Greens' current membership and polling numbers, with a conceivable if narrow pathway for a figure like Burnham to regain 5 per cent or so from both Greens and Reform, and hit a 30 per cent polling which could be enough to carry a majority under first past the post in current conditions.

But such a Labour leadership will no longer fully satisfy a segment of the electorate whose horizons have been broadened. "Corbynism created a mass expectation of political representation," explains Michael Chessum, who was active in Labour under Corbyn and is now an elected Green councillor. "There was a serious project within reach of government, and millions of people wanted it to win. They were never going to be satisfied by a soft-left leader sometime in the 2030s." The combination of heightened expectations and plummeting living standards has created the conditions for a more permanently fragmented and polarised electorate, with a much stronger natural base for Polanski's Greens. Corbyn's Labour squeezed the Greens to just 1.6 per cent of the vote in the 2017 general election.[79] It is difficult to imagine even the most leftmost programme of any plausible Labour leader having the same effect in 2029. Having been a modest precursor to Corbynism, the Greens are now the inheritors of its expansive legacy.

For a period of time, it seemed like Your Party posed a direct challenge to this political space. During Polanski's leadership campaign, it certainly felt as if it had the potential to blow Polanski's prospects to smithereens – for about 40 minutes or so. But following the well-documented catalogue of incompetencies and political failures, Your Party now trails the Greens on almost every relevant metric of polling, often acutely so. In November 2025, YouGov revealed that the Greens led Your Party among some of the key demographics to which many said they could better appeal: more than twice as popular among people in the North, on low incomes, and who voted Leave.[80] In the first national poll which included Your Party as an option, published by Find Out Now in February 2026, Your Party secured less than 1 per cent relative to the Greens' 18 per cent (putting them in second place behind Reform).[81] For better or worse, Your Party shows no sign of being, or wanting to become, the mass party of majoritarian politics which some of its leading proponents once promised to be.

No matter who leads the Labour Party, the upper reaches of any party's ambition for the 2029 election must currently be about a third of the electorate. With Your Party effectively non-functioning, the Greens stand as the only viable electoral project to the left of Labour, something for which there is now an undeniable and solid constituency within the country, with a floor far above the diminutive results they achieved in general elections contested by Corbyn. The Greens of 2026 are in a position of much greater strength relative to 2015, and are surging in a much more dynamic – and potentially permanent – reconfiguration of the political landscape. This makes Polanski's Greens much more resilient to the sort of shock inflicted upon the Greens' last surge by Corbynism ten years ago. Indeed, in the mid-2020s, Polanski *is* the shock.

Corbyn wasn't the only rock against which the Green surge crashed, however. The other, much less discussed, problem of the rapid membership growth in 2015 was that the party was nowhere near institutionally robust enough to absorb, let alone put to good use, the rapid influx of new members. The website just about coped with the peak of 3,000 new members a day but, Bennett reflects now,

> what we didn't have was support for local parties. The same five blokes and a dog who were meeting at the local pub for 10 years suddenly had 40 people turn up to their meetings from all sorts of different backgrounds, and knowledge and experience. The dog probably enjoyed it, but the five men didn't know what to do about it.

This organisational capacity to capitalise on growth and success is just as important as the ability to find and occupy political space. It is almost a blessing that Corbynism didn't allow the Green Party to be undermined by its own inability to absorb this support in the medium term, with the drop in membership and polling acting almost as a pressure valve, allowing the party to grow at a more sustainable pace in the long run. The Greens have come a long way in the ten years since. They've professionalised, developed a full staff structure, provided training and support for local parties, and built a broader base of real power in the country. All the same, the present near-quadrupling of membership from around 60,000 to 225,000 certainly represents a new challenge for the party in terms of ensuring local branches are not overwhelmed while also enabling as many of these members as possible to be active participants in a political project rather than passive supporters.

"It's been a huge step forward and it's largely been incredibly positive, because of the immense amount of energy and enthusiasm," Polanski says. "And I think the party, including members who have been around a long time, have been noticeably welcoming and generous and flexible in the way that they do things, and have been willing to learn new ideas as well as maintain the traditions."

"But we've been building the plane while we've been flying it," he admits.

> A lot of things from vetting candidates to giving them quality training and getting them out door-knocking. There's loads of lessons to be learned, and I think that's fine. Considering we had our most successful election results ever, and we won in Gorton and Denton. I've got no regrets about it, but there are definitely learnings about how to keep improving.

Chapter 7 will return to the question of realising the full potential of a mass membership Green Party.

By the backend of 2019, it was quite obvious that the projects of Corbynism and Remain were – in their own ways, and together – both heading for absolute catastrophe, with a Conservative prime minister enjoying the full consolidation of Leave support from the respectable face of little England to outright street fascists, while Remain support fragmented across a number of parties. Disaster awaited. In the general election of that December, the Conservatives won a landslide majority and Labour were punished by the collapse of their voter base, which had been split down the middle by Brexit. In many ways, of course, this result was one of the regular distortions of the first-past-the-post voting system. Labour had rebuilt its own dismal national polling from mere months prior to achieve 40 per cent in the general election, squeezing the Greens with a new, radical environmental message in addition to the established political offer of a decisive break from Thatcherism. Nowhere did the modest surge of support for Remain or climate take any Green candidate over the line in constituencies other than Brighton Pavilion. The Greens ended the decade where they began: with Caroline Lucas alone in the House of Commons.

The epilogue to this period of Conservative rule will be explored in more detail in Chapter 6 – the 2024 breakthrough in Parliament, rooted in a parallel story beginning in 2019, which saw the Greens deliver a ground game that enabled them to win almost anywhere. In this short period of time the Greens' more or less quadrupled their number of councillors by employing a strategy which would propel an additional three Green MPs into the Commons on the day the Conservatives fell into free-fall. This electoral success would form the basis of Ramsay and Chowns' pitch to the membership in 2025.

Looking back on the 2010s, you can see the seeds of Polanski's leadership beginning to germinate. Most materially in the radically reconstituted membership which, despite the deluge of members to Labour under Corbyn, still remained significantly higher than it was at the start of the decade – with these new members being primarily composed of anti-austerity millennials. But further resonances with Polanski can be heard through these ten years. The Greens gained ground when they were able to move into political space vacated to the left of Labour, and when they used that ground to outline a proud, principled and consistent position on the foremost issue of the day – from austerity to Brexit. They spotted opportunity without being cynically opportunistic. The communications style made a moral and emotional appeal to people's values, while striking an insurgent tone which rallied against a moribund and homogenous establishment. Perhaps most importantly of all, the Greens helped expand the outer boundaries of political possibility and showed millions that there was an alternative to the narrow neoliberal consensus shared by the main parties of the political establishment. All of this would later be embodied – albeit much improved upon – in Polanski's leadership.

Looking at the Greens in the broader context of the political landscape following the 2008 crash, Polanski emerges as more of a continuity candidate for the party than he is a deviation from its past. Still, many continue to claim that the Green Party has moved away from its true and former purpose. But if not with the election of Polanski, when did this rupture occur? Was Bennett the break from the party's more narrowly ecological tradition? Caroline Lucas? Someone or something before that? Or could it be that the potential for ecosocialism reaches right back to the roots of the party?

4

The Roots

In the early days of Polanski's leadership, a lot of the mainstream media made clear that it had little understanding of the constitutional role of the leader of the Green Party of England and Wales, nor how policies and positions were arrived at within its democratic structures. People assumed that the Greens mirrored the rules and conventions of the establishment parties, so Green policies were presented (and parodied) as if they had been produced via focus group for Polanski's leadership launch as something to give to journalists to splash in the newspapers. In reality, every Green policy has been previously established democratically by the membership.

Take the wealth tax, with which Polanski is now closely associated. He did not arrive at this policy personally. A "wealth tax" is called for as "a means of limiting large accumulations of wealth" in a Green Party manifesto published long before Polanski's leadership.[82] In fact, the above brief quotation predates Polanski's *birth* by seven years, being taken from the manifesto which the Green Party (then known as the Ecology Party) put to the electorate in 1975. Nearly 50 years later, this policy would find more sophisticated expression in the 2024 general election manifesto, calling for a tax of 1 per cent on assets exceeding £10 million and 2 per cent exceeding £1 billion.[83] This is the backbone of Polanski's communications on wealth taxes today. But the principle behind this policy can be traced back to the earliest platforms of the party. The same can be said of many of the flagship positions taken by the Greens in the present day, from universal basic income to a principled commitment to devolution.

Founded in the early 1970s, the Green Party is one of the youngest major parties in the UK. Discounting the Liberal Party's merger with the Social Democratic Party in the late 1980s to form the Liberal Democrats (the Liberal Party itself dating back to the 1800s), the only younger party is Reform UK. Given the Greens' less than 60-year history, you might expect to see a fairly unbroken arc of political philosophy and positioning. But that is rarely how the party is discussed, presented instead as if it has undergone at least one if not several fundamental metamorphoses in that relatively short time. For some it is a point of pride. Others claim that the party has been diverted from some imagined former purpose.

Finding that original purpose is like chasing the end of a rainbow, continuing to recede no matter how far you chase it into the party's history. You don't find it just before Polanski becomes leader. You don't find it in the anti-austerity inflection of the 2010s. You don't find it in the 2000s, the 1990s or even the 1980s. The reality is that, following the moment of its founding, the party almost immediately coheres into a form which is recognisably connected to today's, with the main pillars of this continuity being the policy platform and the democratic structures. From the earliest years of the Greens, you can draw an unbroken line from these fundamentals to the eventual leadership of Zack Polanski.

There is no point in pretending otherwise. There were some distinctly rightwing people present at the formation of the Green Party. The most notorious of such figures was undoubtedly Teddy Goldsmith, who sat among a family of notable Tories and high financiers. His father was a Conservative MP, his brother was a billionaire financier, and two of his nephews are Zac and Ben Goldsmith, the former a well-known Conservative politician, the latter a blend of financier and environmentalist, who was, in January 2026, approached by Reform UK to be an environmental adviser. Nonetheless, as the primary author of the seminal *Blueprint for Survival* published in 1972 and founder of the associated Movement for Survival, Teddy Goldsmith undoubtedly lays claim to being one of the forefathers of the Green Party of England and Wales, providing the basis of much of the philosophical foundation of the party.

Goldsmith's *Blueprint* began with the claim that "the principal deficit of the industrial way of life with its ethos of expansion is that it is not sustainable".[84] Thereafter, one of the core arguments it develops remains one of the central distinguishing claims of Green thought to this day, which is that there can be no infinite growth nor infinite extraction on a finite planet. His argument, however, is rooted in the tradition of deep ecology, a concept coined by the Norwegian philosopher Arne Naess, inspired in part by the seminal *Silent Spring* by Rachel Carson. Deep ecologists, such as Goldsmith, argued that traditional ecology sought to protect the environment primarily for the benefit of humankind, rather than in recognition of nature's inherent value. Undoubtedly, contemporary Green politics owes a debt to such admirable recognition of nature's intrinsic worth along with the desire to treat the root causes, rather than symptoms, of ecological problems. But such a philosophy did, however, undoubtedly find close association with socially conservative views, most notably spilling into an outright misanthropy which viewed humans as little more than a problem the wider ecosystem would be better off without. One of the ways this manifests in deep ecological thought is a fixation on population, and, indeed, a reference to the "present increases in human numbers" finds its way onto the very first page of the introduction to the *Blueprint* and remains a preoccupation through the text.

Many leftwing traditions have subsequently criticised deep ecology's focus on the raw numbers of human population and its flattening of "humankind" into a single agent with equally distributed responsibility for environmental destruction. Put most plainly, not everyone is equally to blame for climate change and nature loss. Contemporary Green thought is more likely to focus attention on the overconsumption of the rich above the so-called overpopulation of the poor. Ecofeminists, for example, have drawn attention to the fact that men are more responsible for environmental destruction than women, and – most notably within the context of Polanski's leadership – ecosocialists argue that capitalism is the root cause of environmental degradation, rather than humans *per se*. This counterargument is perhaps most forcefully found in the writings of another foundational Green thinker, Murray Bookchin, an anarchist who advocated for a competing theory of "social ecology" which suggests that environmental degradation is the product of exploitative social relations. This strain of thought has found more recent expression through writers like Jason W. Moore arguing that the term "Anthropocene" (the period of geological time which can be characterised by observable human activity) ought to be renamed the "Capitalocene" (recognising that the observable geological characteristics are in fact the product of industrial capitalism specifically).

Teddy Goldsmith leaned into the reactionary tendencies of deep ecology, associating himself at one point with the far-right movement Nouvelle Droite in France, to the disgust of much of the ecology movement in the UK. But he was far from the only person associated with wealth and rightwing politics present at the origins of the Green Party. In the same year that the *Blueprint* was published, a *Playboy* interview with an expert on the so-called problem of overpopulation inspired a group of professionals to self-organise and discuss such matters, four of whom thereafter came together to form PEOPLE – the political party known today as the Green Party of England and Wales. One of these four founders, and first chair of the party, was a solicitor and former Conservative councillor named Tony Whittaker – noted at the time for his critique of socialism. PEOPLE and Teddy Goldsmith's Movement for Survival then formally merged in 1974, before resolving to change their name to the Ecology Party in 1975.

It was at around this time that the party pivoted from being a small association of organisations and individuals and enjoyed its first small wave of membership. It is from this point, also, that the party begins to acquire its recognisably left-leaning identity. As we saw in Chapter 2, during the leadership election of 2025, a source associated with Ramsay and Chowns' campaign complained that a modest influx of leftwing people (on that occasion, with views and aims largely indistinguishable from the existing membership) felt like a "hostile takeover". This was far from the first time that this had happened. As early as the mid-1970s, the party experienced its first such crisis of confidence among some of its small-c conservatives, as a fledgling membership was perceived to be too leftwing for some of its founding figures.

Jean Lambert is a notable figure for having joined the party in 1977 – during this first wave of growth – and thereafter playing frontline roles (including co-chair and principal speaker) until as recently as 2019, when she stepped down as the MEP for London, a position which she had held for 20 years, since its creation in 1999. Joining at the age of 27, she describes herself as having been a "Left-Liberal" at the time, and had never been a member of a political party before. One of her earliest memories of the party was being down on Teddy Goldsmith's farm for a party meeting and writing out details of the London membership by hand (50 strong, of about 500 total, in those days). Speaking to me in 2026 at the age of 75, she remains deeply engaged with contemporary politics, deftly discussing the pernicious effects of figures like Andrew Tate and Elon Musk today while reminiscing about the earliest days of the Green Party.

"Our early party positioning was very much about contrasting the Greens with the other parties," she tells me, "with the others like some sort of amorphous block. While they had many policy differences, they nevertheless had a great number of things in common. But we said that the question of the environment – planetary security – really ought to be shaking the foundations of politics."

Lambert concedes that there were rightwing elements in the party at its inception, albeit caveating that by saying that at no point was there any conventionally rightwing tendency on the economy, such as support for deregulation in favour of big business. Instead, the flashpoints focussed on some of the regressive hallmarks of deep ecology: migration, population and to what extent ecological politics required coercion. The view held by deep ecologists that "humanity" is to blame for environmental degradation naturally leads to the belief that human behaviour (and indeed numbers) must simply be controlled. This was an ascendant view among many associated with Teddy Goldsmith's Movement for Survival. Social ecology, by contrast, points to the need to transform social relations. This is the tradition which would decisively carry the party forward. "Particular individuals had more of the Movement for Survival idea of asking how almost militarist you would need to be," Lambert remembers. "But they weren't the key figures taking us into the 1980s."

Almost immediately, she argues, the prospectus of the party takes a shape which is recognisably the predecessor of today's, with the more misanthropic foundational tendencies of the party displaced by a growing, more leftward membership (of which Lambert is emblematic) and a politics which valued democracy and egalitarianism above hierarchy and control. What the Greens always offered, in Lambert's view, was a

> critique of economic growth as *the* measure, *the* goal, *the* means to success. And we offered a critique of what the impact of that sort of thinking actually was both on the planet, but also on *people*. We have a finite amount of resources, how do we make the best use of that and share it as equitably as we can?

By the mid-1980s, the nascent political philosophy of the Greens was developed enough to be explored at book length. One of the most well-known figures of the early years of the Green Party, Jonathon Porritt, had just finished a second term as chair of the party when he published *Seeing Green* in 1984 – a text which is cited by Caroline Lucas as one of her entry points into the Green movement and can be seen as something of a bridge from the deep ecology of the party's earliest foundation to a more practical application of progressive politics reflecting the leftward drift of the assembling membership. Here, Porritt evidences just how early into the life of the party its leading figures had a grasp on the interconnectedness of social, economic and environmental policy. "Concern for the environment provides as good a starting point for any green politics," he writes. "But unless it then encompasses fundamental social and economic issues, it will have contributed little towards eliminating the root causes of that crisis."[85]

Despite being full of such things which Polanski might say nearly word for word today, Porritt's book is nonetheless indebted to some of the strains of deep ecology that characterised the party's founding. Most notably, he echoes the fundamental critique of "industrialism" present in the *Blueprint*, and in doing so lumps together both socialism and capitalism as two manifestations of this broader ideology. To be sure, Porritt's critique of capitalism is more forceful than anything which would be found among the mainstream of his contemporary Labour movement. "Capitalism as we know it," he writes, "simply cannot provide the preconditions for an ecologically sane, humane economy."[86] But this is counterbalanced by an equally weighted mistrust of socialism: "Irrespective of who owns the means of production, the unrelenting pursuit of growth and industrial expansion must necessarily degrade the planet and impoverish its people," he argued. "Socialisation of the means of production makes little difference: what are vices under capitalism do not become virtues under communism."[87]

It would be fair to say that the primary basis of Porritt's criticism here was the actually existing socialism of the Soviet Union, which is certainly widely regarded as being an environmental disaster. On this point, Porritt would find little argument among contemporary ecosocialists, who do not view socialism as a silver bullet solution to the ecological crisis but recognise that displacing the profit motive from our economy is a necessary precondition of curbing environmental destruction. "Nationalised industry does not guarantee justice or decarbonisation through economic planning," writes Chris Saltmarsh in his anti-capitalist book on climate justice *Burnt*, "but it allows for the possibility. Privatisation, on the other hand, is an immutable blockage."[88] Porritt is right to critique an "industrialism" which relies on perpetual extraction, consumption and waste. He is also right to recognise that capitalism is simply incapable of transcending this death spiral. But just because the centralised, industrial socialism of the 1980s had not yet escaped it either, it's wrong to conclude that socialism (which does not share capitalism's *inherent* need to accumulate) is simply incapable of becoming the basis of an ecologically balanced society. On the contrary, only democratic control of our economy can offer any potential deviation from the subordination of everything to the fantasy of perpetual economic growth.

For all this, Porritt represents something of a watershed transitional figure for the Greens: blending some elements of deep ecology (including unreformed views on population which he still holds today) with a more practical and more plausibly popular sort of politics which is recognisably left of centre. On balance, Porritt faces towards the contemporary Greens far more than he looks back to the primitivism of a deep ecologist like Goldsmith. In the early 1970s, for example, he was among a group of people who set up the Socialist Environmental Resources Association alongside other leftwing PEOPLE members, publishing works by the likes of the socialist writer Raymond Williams. Porritt has also shown a lifelong commitment to a range of radical and socially progressive campaigns, such as being more than once arrested in 2025, at the age of 74, for defying the proscription of Palestine Action.[89] This is something with which you would struggle to imagine the deep ecologists of the Movement for Survival concerning themselves.

If you focus on the individuals associated with the formation and earliest years of the Green Party, you will undoubtedly find some outrightly rightwing views in the form of the misanthropy and Malthusianism associated with deep ecology. The overt focus on "survival" in the early years explicitly shunned class politics (replacing class interest with species interest) while simultaneously *revealing* their own class interest: a politics partly emerging from the worry that the privileges they enjoyed as upper-class people in the late twentieth century might be terminated by social collapse just over the horizon. Nonetheless, their legacy to Polanski and ecosocialists today is threefold.

Firstly, from the earliest years, the political philosophy of the Greens was always systemic in nature, and the party was never a narrowly interested conservationist pressure group, no matter what the contemporary rightwing press might now imagine. Above all else, they drew attention to the fundamental unsustainability of perpetual economic growth. "Economic growth is supported by unlimited consumption of renewable and non-renewable resources," reads the 1975 Manifesto for a Sustainable Society. "However, in a finite world there is not an infinite supply of natural resources."[90] If the Greens have made just one transformative contribution to political discourse – and one which does indeed transcend orthodoxies on both the left and the right – it is this. Under the early influence of deep ecology, this critique was expressed mainly in terms of industrial activity blasting through hard environmental limits. Over time, however, this insight provided the basis for a more sophisticated social critique: that gains in economic growth do not lead to equally distributed rises in living standards. We are trashing our natural world in service of enriching a small elite of profiteers.

Secondly, whether as deep ecologists or ecosocialists, the

Greens have always offered a more deep-rooted critique of capitalism than any other major electoral forces, such as the mainstream of the Labour Party. As James Schneider has put it, "the [Labour] party does not, as a rule, critique the capitalist system as such, nor its elite beneficiaries. Instead, it seeks to undermine the public's trust in the Conservatives' ability to manage the system effectively, while simultaneously building trust in Labour's ability to do the same."[91] While the Greens have historically been lacking in setting out much actual strategy for transcending capitalism, they do not imagine themselves as being merely the most effective managers of capitalism in the way that Labour has for most of its history – never more so than in recent decades. "In practice," argues Eunice Goes, "this meant a commitment to guaranteeing the survival of capitalism."[92] By contrast, in his 1978 book *The Stable Society*, even Teddy Goldsmith argued explicitly that capitalism's reliance on economic growth makes it incompatible with ecological principles.[93]

Thirdly, those early Greens set the framework of a deeply democratic organisation which was more responsive to its membership than any of the established parties, to a degree that remains badly understood by anyone more accustomed to the larger parties of today. The very first policy outlined in their 1975 manifesto was a political commitment to decentralisation and devolution of power: "Decision making and financial control should be kept as near the personal level as possible," it reads, "and where requirements of coordination and fairness require large-scale decision making, this must be made with the fullest possible democratic participation."[94] This theme remains central to succeeding publications, with the 1979 general election manifesto promising to "consistently apply the golden rule of decentralisation – that nothing should be done at a higher level which can be done at a lower level. Participation is the key to success in any democracy."[95] And, in 1983, a commitment to "legislate for the radical devolution of many powers away from Westminster. So many people today find themselves unable to control their own lives through their own efforts. We must restore that power to the community and to the individual."[96] It is this, rather than a conventional environmentalism *per se*, which is arguably the more foundational and enduring political aim of the Greens. So central was it to the DNA of Green politics that it was encoded into the structures of the party itself. This, perhaps above all else, is ecosocialism's most valuable inheritance of the deep ecologists.

At the Green Party's autumn conference of 2025, the first in which Zack Polanski attended as leader, a motion was passed by the name of "Abolish Landlords". Owing to a combination of the provocative name and the heightened attention conferred upon the Greens by Polanski's win, this was widely reported upon by the mainstream press and derided by establishment figures. "Wacky", was the assessment of Secretary of State responsible for housing, Steve Reed, on the *New Statesman* podcast, asking (and surely he could not have been posing this question literally) "if you abolish landlords, where are you going to get the homes from?"[97] As with the wealth tax, implicit to much of this coverage was the assumption that this motion was a gimmick dreamed up by the people around Polanski to drum up some attention during his first party conference. In reality, Polanski had almost nothing to do with it.

Unlike in most parties where the flagship policy emanating from conference is workshopped by wonks in lanyards and focus-grouped to oblivion, Abolish Landlords was conceived by a barista on the outer city limits of Brighton. That is to say, an ordinary member of the Green Party. Alexander Sallons sat for a coffee with another local party member, Martin Farley (who has been a member of the party's tax and fiscal policy working group), where they set out their thinking around the logical implication of much of the existing party policy on housing. Inspired by works like Nick Bano's *Against Landlords* (arguing that landlordism is the primary cause of the housing crisis), the motion was not to bluntly criminalise landlordism should the Greens achieve state power. It was simply to observe that the economic carrots and sticks contained in the party's housing policy would have the effect of disincentivising landlordism, tending towards effective abolition over time. Such policies included rent controls, the cessation of right-to-buy and buy-to-let mortgages, a land value tax, and a mass expansion of council housing – all of which would erode the profitability of private landlordism while strengthening a state response to the housing crisis. The idea was to bring all of this existing policy together in a motion which made the implicit effect of all this policy an explicit intention.

Any member can submit a motion to be considered by conference, and all members vote on the prioritisation ballot which determines the order in which motions are heard (and which are therefore likely to actually be voted on in practice, given the finite length of a conference). Any member can attend a conference to vote, and their vote would carry exactly the same weight as Zack Polanski's. A body called the Standing Orders Committee

(SOC) is ultimately responsible for making sure all motions and processes follow party rules and so on, so there is some agreed authority to ensure that proceedings are constitutional and have legitimacy. But the leader, as an individual, has no bearing on these processes whatsoever, and cannot control, manage or flatly ignore the membership as other party leaders can. This was the process through which Abolish Landlords ended up being heard at the autumn conference of 2025. There was some marginalised dissent to the proposal on the day (mainly on grounds of the explicit foregrounding of class antagonism among a minority of members), but the motion was carried with an overwhelming majority after a spirited discussion on the conference floor. "The Private Rental Sector has failed," read the successful motion. "It is a vehicle for wealth extraction, funnelling money from Renters to the Landlord Class. This motion makes it clear Green Party policy is to seek the effective abolition of Private Landlordism and our support for building Council Housing."[98]

This episode exemplifies three things. The first is that this is another example of the plainly leftwing composition of the party membership. The second is the true sovereignty of conference as the supreme decision-making body within the party, and how that means that the members are much stronger than any elected leader. The third is to note the ability to use motions at conference for a dual purpose: primarily of course to ensure that the Greens have a programme of policy for which they can advocate and put into practice wherever they achieve power. But Abolish Landlords also points to the campaigning and communicative possibilities of policies being used to spark constructive debate, inflame useful antagonisms and have inherent political purpose. This was, self admittedly by the motion's authors, part of the point of the exercise.

Conference is just one facet of the party which is constituted to create a more democratic body than other UK parties. The party is governed by two main bodies: the Green Party Council (GPC) and the Green Party Executive (GPEx). GPC is a council of 36 party members who are responsible for the political strategy and direction of the party, and ultimately responsible for its governance. Any member who has been in the party more than two years is eligible to stand under its single transferable vote elections, although there are provisions to ensure that there is sufficient spread of representation across the regions of England and Wales, and that there is minimum representation of the global majority. GPEx is responsible for the day-to-day running of the party and the execution of the political strategy set by GPC. (Subordinate to all of this is a conventional staffing structure, helmed by a CEO.) Polanski, as the leader of the Green Party, sits on both of these bodies, with the same voting rights as any other member of the body. In this sense, it calls to mind how Polanski has exactly the same voting rights as ordinary members at a conference. Contrary to the all-powerful behemoth that he is sometimes presented as being in the mainstream media, akin to a traditional party leader, the Greens' structures place very firm limits on the leader's hard power. In this way, party democracy can even be read as a prefigurative form of politics, embedding the principles of decentralisation and devolution from its political philosophy into its constituted structures.

How the internal party democracy operates in practice when Greens are actually wielding state power is a largely untested question. Some tensions can be anticipated. One is already at play in principle, which is that the Party has no whips (party officials appointed to ensure that MPs vote in line with the party's position and interests). This is commonly presented as being another admirable example of the Greens' pioneering democratic approach: putting into Parliament a cohort of independently minded people who won't be used as warm bodies to mindlessly vote one way or another. In this there is much to admire. On the other side of the coin, it raises the question of the power and the purpose of a party manifesto if all elected representatives are effectively free to ignore it. For most of the party's recent past – with one MP in the chamber – the Greens have, to say the least, managed to avoid splits in its parliamentary party. This may not endure forever, especially if Polanski returns dozens of new Greens in 2029.

The prospect of Greens actually entering into some sort of power-sharing arrangement presents even bigger questions: can members veto coalitions? Choose ministers? Hold elected officials to their commitments? Responding to such questions, Polanski himself draws a useful parallel with the Scottish Greens, who in 2021 had the opportunity to share power with the Scottish National Party (SNP) in the Scottish Parliament. The so-called Bute House Agreement – a pact of cooperation involving coordination on certain policy areas, the appointment of Green ministers, and confidence-and-supply support on votes – was negotiated by the leaders of both parties. Crucially, however, it could not be ratified or implemented from the Greens' perspective without the majority support of Scottish Green members, and two-thirds of their elected council. Polanski points to this model of internal democracy as the sort of guardrails which could support and scrutinise elected leadership in the event of some form of power-sharing arrangement becoming possible in England and Wales.

One partial resolution to all of these tensions is the trump card of the membership: open selections. Local branches are fully in control of whether they stand in any given electoral contest, and who they put forward if so. Greens do not share the privilege, enjoyed by the elected politicians in other parties, of being automatically entitled to defend their seat in any subsequent public election. Every time a Green wants to be re-elected to public office, they require the renewed mandate from members of their local branch to be a candidate in national and local elections. This means that if an elected Green deviates from agreed priorities, policies or principles, there is an extremely robust and effective way in which they can be held to account by their local members: denying them the right to run next time and selecting another candidate in their place.

Compare these power relations within the Greens with the atrophying democratic culture of Labour. As Andrew Murray has observed:

> the question of the proper relationship of the PLP (Parliamentary Labour Party) to the wider party has been answered in practice – near-complete autonomy. The party can formulate whatsoever policy it likes, but its decisions can never be more than advisory. The parliamentary leadership alone determines what may be implemented and what discarded ... answering to a phantom "national

> interest" of which the movement from which it springs is a subordinate fraction.[99]

This was most recently well evidenced by the 2022 motion to include proportional representation as a manifesto commitment. No such commitment can be found in the 2024 manifesto.

This is not a bug of Starmerism but a feature of the Labour Party. Even under Corbyn, who had the stated aim of democratising the party, the prevailing logics and structures of Labour dragged its would-be reformist leaders towards a culture of command and control and instilled a suspicion of ceding power to members. "The Labour Party changed us much more than we changed the Labour Party," was Michael Chessum's assessment. "We came out of Corbynism with no open selections, no sovereign conference, no meaningful democratisation of the party at all."

Your Party had a stated aspiration to build a uniquely democratic party within British politics. Its foundational months were characterised by two competing visions for the party, figureheaded by Jeremy Corbyn and Zarah Sultana, respectively. Corbyn's camp could be characterised as essentially desiring to replicate Labour Party Corbynism, including what its internal critics characterise as mistakes: overcentralisation, tight control and a suspicion of membership democracy. Sultana, for her part, advocated for "maximum member democracy", which is usually expressed as "one member, one vote": a principle that has been adopted by the Greens since its founding. In any event, it was to be Corbyn's camp which won the Central Executive Committee elections in February 2026, along with Corbyn being installed as *de facto* leader as the parliamentary spokesperson. In spite of the thriving culture of democratic participation evidenced by the turnout in internal elections, Your Party is now widely regarded as being subject to the same democratic deficits as Corbyn's Labour.

We return, then, to the founding of a party. For the Greens, to the faint embarrassment of the sort of people making arguments like mine, this was broadly speaking a handful of the petty bourgeoisie with some fairly socially reactionary views sat around a kitchen table, bolstered by Tories and high financiers. For many of the people associated with Your Party in particular, the desirability of a party to be founded and constituted by socialists with the aim of socialism explicitly stated is presented as if it were some sort of iron-clad guarantee of the party's purpose forever. For what it's worth, Labour's 1918 constitution was heralded as the "birth of a socialist party" by the *Manchester Guardian*, and even Blair's infamous rewrite of Clause IV of the Labour Rule Book begins with the explicit claim (absent in its original wording, incidentally) that "The Labour Party is a democratic socialist party."[100] But few socialists would agree that the Labour Party is a socialist party today, not least because, if it were, there would be no need to set up a new one. Things change. The reality is that political parties are themselves unavoidably a terrain of contest and political struggle, and are not any one fixed or unchanging thing in particular. Presently, the Green Party can lay claim to the following attributes: a foundational critique of capitalism; a radically social democratic and socialist body of policy; a thriving tendency of socialists within an avowedly leftwing membership; a democratic structure which empowers these members; and an ability to win elections across the country. It also has a capable and aligned leader in the form of Zack Polanski.

In the long view of the party's full history, Polanski himself is arguably one of the less important ingredients of the Green Party's ability to be an effective vehicle for ecosocialism. Without question, he has had an electrifying impact on the party's material success, but the roots of his leadership go into much deeper soil: the composition of the membership, and the way in which they are empowered by the democratic structures of the party. The mainstream reaction to Polanski's leadership has been to portray him as if he has wrested the controls of the party and wrenched it in a new direction. This is a fatal misreading which leads many political opponents to a false conclusion: that the removal of Polanski will restore the Greens to their "correct" place in the UK political landscape; once again marginalised, neutered and enjoying their allotments. Undoubtedly, the need to find a successor to Polanski, and a wider team of effective political communicators and operators, is a live strategic question for the Greens, as well as the need to build further organisational resilience at the grassroots. But this mainstream analysis fails to recognise the much deeper currents which have allowed Polanski to surf the crest of his wave.

The real power of the Greens lies not in its leader but its membership. The true threat to the hegemony of establishment parties is not Polanski but the significant, consistent and growing proportion of the public which wants a decisive break from neoliberalism, a constituency now given organised expression in the form of a thriving and surging Green Party of England and Wales. In other words: a reconstituted 99 per cent. If political opponents persuade themselves that by taking out Zack Polanski they will bring the Green Party to its knees, the Greens will simply slip through the fingers of their clenched fists, leaving them grasping at air.

Part II

5

Is the Green Party *Really* Leftwing?

Some people have difficulty placing the Greens on the traditional left–right political spectrum. In fairness, a lot of this difficulty has been created by Greens themselves. Figures throughout the movement's history have deliberately tried to break free of this paradigm and define Green political philosophy as something entirely its own, with a notorious expression of this impulse being that Greens were "not left, nor right, but forward".

To give due credit to the Greens who want to transcend the left–right axis, it is true to say that Greens are undoubtedly offering a politics distinct from almost all of the actually existing leftwing projects of the twentieth century, and most of the imagined ones too. As the cliché (nearly) goes, real ecosocialism has never been tried. But the practical pursuit of Green politics has always tended towards egalitarianism and democracy rather than a belief in natural hierarchies and authoritarianism. And the traditional political spectrum still holds real descriptive power over the defining aims of the Greens: achieving common ownership of key resources; maximising democratic participation through society and the economy; and liberation for marginalised and oppressed people, to name but three. All of this is recognisably leftwing.

In Chapter 4, I argued that – in spite of the rightwing tendencies associated with the politics of deep ecology at the foundations of the party – the potential for ecosocialism was encoded into the structure and the culture of the Greens from the start. The decades since have seen that potential increasingly realised through a process of the party becoming more self-consciously and self-identifiably left. Perhaps the most obvious staging post along the way was the leadership of Natalie Bennett, described in Chapter 3; her clear anti-austerity platform adopted a self-consciously leftwing inflection with an implicit class analysis. Today we have an explicitly class-based politics articulated under the leadership of Polanski.

As this chapter will describe, the Greens' current day positioning as a self-defined, proudly leftwing party has been the product of a consistent process of development over decades, rather than the result of occasional seismic ruptures visited by particular leaders or events. Juxtaposing Jonathon Porritt with Caroline Lucas provides an illustrative example of this evolution. These are two strongly aligned figures, similar in background, presentation and outlook. But while Porritt went to great lengths to disavow the actually existing socialism of the Soviet Union in the 1980s, when *Guardian* journalist Owen Jones 40 years later asked Lucas whether she was a socialist in 2015, she gave a one-word answer: "definitely".[101]

For Natalie Bennett, a leftwing analysis of the ecological emergency is unavoidable. "It is impossible to be a philosophically coherent rightwing Green," she argues. You can have an instinctive concern for the environment, especially as a conservationist, and still hold rightwing views. But any serious analysis of the overlapping environmental crises leads you to leftwing solutions. That's because "in the UK, we use our share of three planets every year", she explains. "If you say, 'right, everyone cut back by two-thirds', that literally leaves a lot of people dead. So it's impossible to have a coherent position that doesn't address economic inequality." Contrary to the claims of the Greens' rightwing critics, environmental politics are not being used disingenuously to advance leftwing causes. It's the other way around. Leftwing politics are being engaged as the only democratic and egalitarian route to realising Green goals.

Ecosocialist Greens identify capitalism itself as the engine of the ecological emergency in which we find ourselves, and hence the root issue which Greens must address. While traditional Marxism has generally been observed to have had too little to say about ecology, modern Marxist thinkers like Jason W. Moore have offered correctives, noting that surplus value is exploitatively extracted from nature as well as workers.[102] Capitalism's need to perpetually extract, produce, consume and pollute in pursuit of profit means it is ultimately incompatible with hard environmental limits; an argument most famously popularised in the subtitle of Naomi Klein's paradigm shifting 2014 book "Capitalism vs. the Climate".[103] Or as Chris Saltmarsh puts it in his book *Burnt*, "the imperative for capital to accumulate at all costs, and the centrality of profit to all economic activity, means that our current economic system offers no incentive for capital and capitalist states to transition from fossil fuels to renewables, let alone protect workers' rights at the same time". More pithily: "as long as profit is supreme, climate change will get much worse".[104]

This ecosocialist strain of thought represents its own tendency within the party and indeed the global leftwing community, perhaps best embodied in the Green Party of England and Wales by Derek Wall, who joined the Greens (then the Ecology Party) in 1980, and went on to be elected as a principal speaker from 2006 to 2008. "As a teenager joining the party," Wall tells me, "I quickly learned that economic growth is a problem. And then I made the link from that to anti-capitalism." From the 1980s onwards, there were socialist and Marxist groups outside of the Greens who helped inform some of its intellectual currents including, as Wall remembers, an obscure Trotskyite splinter group called Socialist Self-Management, which counted among its ranks a youthful Keir Starmer.[105] At the same time, the composition of the party membership continued to drive left. While the rightward lurch of Starmer's Labour is credited with the explosion of Green membership today, Wall points out that the Greens have always been the natural beneficiaries of Labour's longer rightward drift from the mid-1980s onwards – from Kinnock's showdown with the left of his party, through the so-called modernisation under New Labour. Only Corbyn's Labour provided a brief reprieve from this broader trend of Labour's move to the right.

In the Greens, the 1980s and 1990s were characterised by "fights" between the ascendant self-described left of the party and "people who are more managerial" as Wall characterises them. These two groups came to be known as the "realos" (short for realists) and the "fundis" (short for fundamentalists, of which Wall was one). "A lot of the radicalism in the Green Party was actually more libertarian and anarchist," Wall remembers. "And this reflects the suspicion that if you have more centralised, managerial, conventional structures, that's then going to turn into something which is more rightwing." The so-called realos argued for (and won) constitutional changes to the party which moderately centralised power in 1991, in service of professionalising the party for a programme called Green 2000 which promised a parliamentary majority by the millennium. Needless to say, in this aim they were not successful. Wall regards Green 2000 as being "ridiculous" and reflects that "the more direct action oriented, left-anarchist kind of thing, that was actually more pragmatic". Here, then, was an early manifestation of the tension between electoralism and activism, which we will further explore in Chapter 7.

In 2006, Wall became one of the party's principal speakers and convened with a small group of party members to form Green Left, founded to explicitly advance ecosocialism within the party, and was for many years the preeminent openly socialist segment of Green Party membership. It still exists today – albeit with diminished membership, and a sense of exhaustion (not helped by a perception of being tainted by some elements of transphobia in its later years). It based itself on the principles found in the Ecosocialist Manifesto of 2001, which stated that:

> In our view, the crises of ecology and those of societal breakdown are profoundly interrelated and should be seen as different manifestations of the same structural forces … Moreover, these underlying forces are essentially different aspects of the same drive, which must be identified as the central dynamic that moves the whole: the expansion of the world capitalist system <add space>…
>
> We believe that the present capitalist system cannot regulate, much less overcome, the crises it has set going. It cannot solve the ecological crisis because to do so requires setting limits upon accumulation – an unacceptable option for a system predicated upon the rule: Grow or Die![106]

In the present day, the newly constituted group Greens Organise (GO) can be seen as an energetic successor to Green Left as well as an immediate precursor to Polanski's leadership. Discussions for the new grouping kicked off just before the 2024 general election with the aim of bringing together the party's ecosocialists into an organised bloc, in service of building an educated, active, mass party of the left which was rooted in the working class. The founding figures were aghast that despite the steady electoral success of the Greens, the party was failing to punch through on the national stage and occupy the political space that was being vacated by an increasingly rightward Labour.

GO is primarily composed of a blend of former Labour leftists who recently departed Starmer's project in disgust, and some of the relative veterans of the anti-austerity 2015 Green surge. The two co-chairs of the steering group are from the former grouping. Steve Jackson joined the party in 2025 with a background in Labour, trade unionism and Extinction Rebellion, and was in Polanski's leadership election campaign team. Hau-Yu Tam is a councillor in Lewisham who was in Labour, until she found her Palestinian ceasefire motion blocked by colleagues in 2023, and subsequently became subject to disciplinary action for organising in solidarity with Palestine (complaints of which she was later cleared). Resigning her membership in 2024, she sat as an independent for some time, campaigning for independents like Jeremy Corbyn, Leanne Mohamad and Andrew Feinstein in the 2024 general election, before being welcomed into the Greens in 2025. This owed itself to outreach efforts from the likes of Robert Magowan, chair of Haringey Green Party (and one of the socialists who stuck around after the 2015 Green surge), who helped her overcome her concerns about the "tone" of the party and what she perceived to be rigidity of thinking around electoralism. Tam was surprised by how much of a home she found in the Greens, who were "so supportive" during an allegation that she violated the International Holocaust Remembrance Alliance (IHRA) definition of antisemitism, brought forward by Labour a few weeks after she defected to the Greens. Such a journey is emblematic of many of the new members who joined the Greens under Polanski.

While supportive of GO, Polanski was not formally involved, nor did GO endorse him in the leadership election of 2025. But the parallels in their aims are stark: better comms, bolder politics. Both GO and Polanski are products of the mainstreaming of leftwing traditions within the party and represent strong contemporary socialist tendencies establishing themselves among both the grassroots and the leadership. With the influx of members following Polanski's election, ready to be organised and mobilised by the likes of GO, and empowered by the party's democratic structures, it's very possible that this tendency is now effectively hegemonic within the party.

That said, there is still huge scope for GO to develop. Firstly, as co-chair Steve Jackson admits, there isn't great representation of GO members in positions of power within the party, such as local party officers, national committee members and so on, and so embedding committed ecosocialists into the party structures is a key future objective for GO. Secondly, neither is there presently a deeply rooted ideological coherence across the party membership. While the majority of members are undoubtedly loosely attached to the sort of politics associated with Polanski and GO, there's a huge potential for political education to sharpen a shared analysis of class, power and collective strategy. This, too, is the sort of thing GO is well placed to undertake. Polanski has not been wizened and forged in the fire of decades of thankless graft for socialism; and his communications style is usually situated within the broadest church of populist leftwing appeal. This is part of his ability to reach a broad audience. But it also creates a need for a body like GO to radicalise, educate and organise the tens of thousands of people coming through the door, and turn them into effective, strategic ecosocialists who can win power. "We've got to get much stronger at electoral strategy," Tam tells me, "Heading towards 2029, we need a candidate support programme. We need candidate identification, incubation and a support network."

There are presently no other factions of any power or organisation – either left or right – which are comparable to the ecosocialists of GO. There are single-issue pressure groups (such as Greens for HS2) and there are identity-based groupings (such as the Young Greens, Greens of Colour and the LGBTIQA+ Greens). But the only notable contemporary, remotely organised rightwing grouping in the party would be the self-styled gender critical Greens who have organised in groups such as Green Women's Declaration. This network of members is known for standing in internal elections on a platform foregrounding the issue of sex-based rights, colluding with the rightwing press and even taking legal action against the party. The influx of members since Polanski's leadership has marginalised these members, and the more misanthropic views of longer-standing deep Greens regarding matters like so-called overpopulation are now also extremely minoritised. Now more than ever, the party is overwhelmingly socially progressive and economically leftwing. Within this membership, an explicitly ecosocialist outlook is in the ascendancy. This is evidenced by the astonishing mandate awarded to Polanski in 2025 – and the many tens of thousands of members which he has since attracted.

What would the advancement of such ecosocialism look like under Polanski? "For me," he says, "it's ultimately about making sure that we're not socialising risks and privatising rewards. We need to be socialising the rewards." The ultimate vision which he sets out contains the traditional hallmarks of a socialist project: devolution of power to workers, democratisation of the economy, shared ownership of common assets and the means of production. To get there, though, he thinks in pragmatic and transitional terms. "Nationalising water is a good example," he tells me.

> Nationalisation is not socialism in and of itself. But I'd say it's a clear step forward in terms of strengthening social democracy and in terms of removing the profit motive from water companies. Socialism is a step you have to take after that, which is about worker control within those water companies. That's something I want to do. But you have to take the first step first.

A proposed "first step" in this particular example can be seen in his capacity as a London Assembly member, pushing the mayor of London, Sadiq Khan, to insist that the mayor has a seat on the board of Thames Water – as is common in many other European countries. This stops far short of even nationalisation, let alone worker control of the company, but stands as an example of a concrete demand which Greens can make to increase democratic oversight of the profiteering companies which control our shared resources. For Polanski, the difference between radical social democracy and socialism is not a hard distinction; both sit on a spectrum along which we are trying to move our politics along, towards a place where the profit motive is eroded, undermined and displaced. "It's about moving in the direction of recognising that our vital assets, the things that we rely on to survive and indeed thrive, shouldn't be run for private profit, and shouldn't be run by corporations who are intent on destroying our planet," he tells me. "They should be run for the good of the many – for the 99 per cent."

One of the big questions still hanging over the Greens' relationship to socialism is their relationship to class. This points to one of the more good-faith difficulties in situating the Greens on the left–right spectrum: that they have no obvious or inherent social base, nor any rooting in notable, legitimising institutions outside of the party, such as trade unions. The evolution of the Greens' shifting consciousness on class – from a historical nadir of actively rejecting class politics – has taken the form of a succession of claims which are all perfectly justified: firstly, that Green policies and manifestos stand to greatly benefit the working class; secondly, that such policies are generally popular among the working classes; thirdly, that more and more working-class people are represented within the party; and, fourthly, that more and more working-class people are actually voting for the party. All of these things are true. What this trajectory arguably stops short of, however, is actually seeing the working class as an agent of political change. Derek Wall writes about this in *The Rise of the Green Left*:

> Green political theory has often been weak when it comes to the question of "agency". This question deals with the issue of which social group or groups are most likely to create change. Greens have often ignored strategic questions in general, with sometimes disastrous results. It is not enough to see change as a product of election victories without a wider process of change. Greens have often seen class as irrelevant. This is because many Greens, but not all, see the working class as unsympathetic to environmental concerns. It is also because Greens believe that all of us, in the end, will be harmed by catastrophic environmental change and thus we all have a potential interest in green political change. "Species" interest replaces specific class interest.[107]

For ecosocialists, workers play a key role within the struggle to transition from capitalism. As Matthew T. Huber puts it, "[the working class's] strategic location at the point of production gives it structural power over the source of capital's profits and social reproduction more generally".[108] This most obviously takes the form of strikes – but it can also take the form of a more proactive participation in the transition from a fossil economy. The most commonly cited example of this from history came in the form of the Lucas Plan, where union members in the Lucas Aerospace Corporation responded to the announcement of deep job cuts in the 1970s by drawing up an active counterproposal to make socially useful products such as wind turbines. Management crushed its implementation, but the episode stands as a blueprint of what could be achieved with requisite worker empowerment and organisation, and the Green traditions of democratisation and devolution of power will aid this endeavour. Hannah Spencer was smeared as somehow not being an authentic plumber when it transpired that her qualifications had allowed her to install heat pumps, which supply homes with low-carbon heating. Less was made of the positive case for Spencer as an emblematic showcase of just the transition which will need to be unleashed within the productive working class: orienting their skills and experience away from environmentally destructive practices which enrich a tiny minority, and towards useful work for the common good of people and planet. A more democratised workforce could be a precondition of an army of Spencers going street to street, insulating homes and hooking people up to clean, cheap heat networks.

The relationship between the Greens and the unions is

strengthening. Straight after Polanski finished his victory speech after being elected leader of the party, he hopped on the tube to get to Bethnal Green, where he met with officers of the United Voices of the World (UVW). The UVW was founded in 2014 by Latin American cleaners and has gone on to become one of the unions (along with the Independent Workers of Great Britain) most notable for organising and representing some of the most precarious and vulnerable workers in the economy: migrants, gig economy workers and people on zero-hours contracts. Polanski himself has a proud track record of showing solidarity with members' disputes, such as his long-standing support of cleaners in Sage Nursing Home who went on strike for a living wage, sick pay and improved conditions. While Starmer was warning his Labour frontbench to stay away from picket lines, Polanski stood with those workers in the falling snow. Joining striking NHS staff at Epsom Hospital, he unexpectedly ended up advocating on behalf of union members directly to the CEO during the board meeting, extracting a commitment to meet the striking workers – which they had hitherto failed to do.

Such solidarity has been rewarded by the union movement during his tenure to date, with the president of the Bakers' Union (BFAWU), Ian Hodson, giving Polanski his best wishes and expressing his hopes for Polanski's victory during the leadership election campaign, to the general secretary of the National Education Union (NEU) sitting down to talk to Polanski on the latter's podcast, *Bold Politics*, and, in turn, inviting him to be the keynote speaker at the union's 2026 conference. These are relatively small gestures, but they are seismic in comparison to anything which has been oriented towards the Greens historically, and very tentatively point towards the possibility of political realignment among organised labour.

The voting intention of NEU members is instructive. In the 2024 general election, 60 per cent of them voted Labour. At the time of polling in January 2026, that was slashed to an abysmal 18 per cent, with the Greens instead being the most popular choice.[109] The idea of the Greens becoming the primary electoral representation of the unions might still feel like a tall mountain to climb. Then again, the thought of the Greens replacing Labour as the primary party of the Left would until very recently itself have been laughable. Things change. Maybe it is time to consider this improbable possibility.

Prior to Polanski, the relationship between the Greens and the unions has been slowly changing over the course of the last ten years or so. The current trade union liaison officers on GPEx, Kate Jones and Paul Valentine, both joined the party in the mid-2010s and recall the "absolutely acerbic" reaction you used to get from some older trade union members when you told them you were in the Greens. Now being a Green in trade union spaces is commonplace. In 2025, there was an "explosion" of new regional trade union liaison officers in the Green Party, and Greens within the rank-and-file membership of unions is becoming increasingly common too. "People are beginning to coalesce in their union groups and realise there's actually like a little caucus of Greens in my Unison branch or my UCU [University and College Union] branch or whatever it might be," Jones says. "Previously, I think people would have been quieter about it or it would have been anomalous – now it's becoming more normal." Valentine and Jones are ready to push this further. "We're getting the Green Party present at every trade union conference we can get to this year," Jones explains.

> We're going to be at the Durham Miners' Gala. We are going to be at the Tolpuddle Festival. We're at the TUC Congress. And we're not just standing for a photo with a placard, we're doing fringe events that means the union members present can talk to us and tell us: what would you like to see from the Green Party?

The Labour Party obviously derives a great deal of its power from unions, most tangibly in the form of affiliation, which pumps money into the party bureaucracy and allows it to operate and compete as a major electoral force. But the organised labour and union movement also bestows Labour much of its historical political legitimacy. At its founding, one of the clear political purposes of the party was to provide electoral representation for trade unionists. This relationship rooted the project in strong social institutions in industrial communities, of which the trade union was the most formally organised. The bonds of this relationship between Labour and labour, however, have been fraying for decades. Most clearly this happened during the New Labour years, in which the link was deliberately weakened by Blair in service of constituting the so-called "political wing of the British people", choosing not to undo the aggressively anti-union legislation of Thatcher.[110] Things have not improved under the Labour government of the present day, which, in turn, has also elected to leave the fundamentals of the Thatcherite industrial relations settlement in place. The status quo of union deference to the party cannot be expected to obtain forever. In late 2025, Unite general secretary Sharron Graham made public remarks about the real possibility of disaffiliating from Labour, on the grounds that affiliation is increasingly difficult to justify to a membership which deplored the direction taken under a Starmer government. In March 2026, she proved she wasn't bluffing, when members voted to cut the fees they paid to the Labour Party by 40 per cent – a sum of over half a million pounds per year – as punishment for the party's failure to adequately support the Birmingham bin strikers.[111] This represents one of the most viable opportunities for political realignment in organised labour for decades.

Can the Greens capitalise? It's true to say that, along with the mistrust some Greens have shown towards the working class in general as outlined by Wall earlier, some of the most persistent scepticism has been reserved for the trade unions, insofar as they can be castigated for aligning themselves with the forces of polluting industry and environmental degradation. There is some legitimacy to this argument, not least evidenced by the likes of GMB persistently going to bat for the fossil fuel industry or aviation expansion.[112] For all its demonised portrayal as a wellspring of Marxist indoctrination, trade unionism – as prosecuted through its leadership – is inflected with a pragmatism and small-c conservatism, principally concerned with the immediate and narrow interests of its members. Often this involves actively propping up the capitalist order. Sometimes this takes the form of seeking to preserve or create jobs in actively destructive industries.

This pragmatism also leads unions to back promising political prospects, however. For the duration of the party's history, the philosophical basis for union affiliation to Labour has been in complete alignment with the pragmatic case – it has for nearly a century been either the official opposition or the government. But within this context, there is evidence to be seen of unions jumping ship to back a winner – most obviously in the 2015 Labour leadership election when it was clear that Corbyn's pro-union platform had a chance of actually being realised when he was on course to win. It is admittedly very hard to imagine circumstances in which the established unions affiliate to the Greens in the medium term. But equally, it is also hard to imagine the status quo persisting in the face of a policy platform which offers mere crumbs to unions and workers, a rank-and-file membership increasingly at odds with the politics of the actually existing party, and – more to the point – a Labour Party reduced to being a minority force in Parliament. At which point the question of Sharon Graham will resound across the movement more loudly: what are we getting for our affiliation?

At the TUC Congress of 2025, Polanski quite understandably showed an openness and willingness to work towards union affiliation with the Greens but first and foremost stressed his immediate-term desire to simply build better (and sincere) relationships with them. For Valentine and Jones, however, the immediate strategic goal is *disaffiliation*. In their view, the more efficient organisation of rank-and-file members, with a growing number of Greens in their midst, are the conditions in which you can imagine memberships agitating for votes on affiliation. Rather than simply replicating the centralised structure of union fiefdom with the Greens standing in for Labour, they see disaffiliation as the precondition for a more democratic, engaged and pluralistic era of union support for political parties and candidates. "If no one's affiliated," argues Valentine,

> it allows unions to focus specifically on issues and candidates. Unions can then go: right, who have we got in this part of the country? All the Greens in Brighton, they can have a load of cash. All the Greens in Bristol, they can have cash. There's an independent who's standing in wherever part of the country, they can have a bit of cash. There's a Your Party candidate over here, and they can have a bit of cash. It allows fluidity and working together, which is what we would advocate as Greens.

From this perspective, one can see the opportunity for the Greens to not only replace Labour as the foremost electoral force on the Left of English politics but to be a central node in a revitalised and re-politicised network of organised labour. A growing number of the preconditions for this look good. Polling following the victory of Hannah Spencer in Gorton and Denton, for example, found the Greens to be the most popular party among *all people of working age*.[113] There is a route to the Green Party laying legitimate claim to being the party of UK workers at the next general election.

On May Day 2026, Polanski held a rally in Manchester People's History Museum (hosting a flagship exhibition celebrating the centenary of the 1926 General Strike) to unveil the Green Party's workers' charter.[114] This amalgamation of the party's pro-worker policies included improvements to pay and conditions, such as a commitment to a £15 minimum wage and more statutory holiday. The most transformative pillar of the charter, however, came in the form of the explicit commitment to building collective power, along with winning and extracting concessions which improve the lives of workers. Most notably this included a pledge to "scrap all anti-union and anti-strike laws introduced since 1979. Bring in strong legal rights to strike, picket and protest, including solidarity action and action for political and social causes." Reforms to improve pay and conditions are the bread and butter of union work. But the promise to upend the Thatcherite (and Blairite) settlement that crushed organised labour holds the potential to transform class power in the UK. An incumbent Labour government hasn't touched this with a barge pole. The Greens, under Polanski, promise to empower the working class as a collective agent of political change. Such empowerment will be pivotal to the successful displacement of an economic system which privileges profit over planet.

The political establishment remains determined to persuade us that class politics is a distortion of the true purpose of the Green Party. By implication, they argue that Green goals could just as plausibly be advanced from the right of politics. Could they be right? After all, it is only fair to concede that traditional conservatism has historically had more to say about the environment than most major leftwing movements of the twentieth century. Perhaps the most quintessential embodiment of high Toryism, the late Roger Scruton wrote an entire book on Green thinking, seeking to situate it in a Burkean tradition of conservatism. In *Green Philosophy*, Scruton writes of

> the importance of small associations [and] autonomous institutions ... gatherings of people that exist for the sake of membership – sometimes, but by no means always, with a common

> purpose – conducting their affairs without interference from the state, and usually without the desire for political prominence. Such associations form the stuff of civil society.[115]

Resonances with these "little platoons", as Edmund Burke called them, can be found in Green thinking from its origins in the 1970s through to its present-day policy platform – in the form of the Greens' philosophical commitment to devolving power to the most local level feasible for any given form of action or decision-making. This arouses the suspicion of leftists who retain a commitment to big states and centralised planning. Such suspicion is not soothed by the form of localism pursued by the actually existing Conservatism of Thatcherism or Cameroonism, the former of which ravaged the country with austerity, stripped local authorities to the bone, and then set them up to fail with a raft of new statutory duties they could not possibly discharge. Along with this, the notorious "big society" enjoined citizens and civil society to step in where the state had stepped back and simply get on with trying to hold their community together with no support or resources. Figures like Jonathon Porritt have sought to distance the Greens from this sort of vision for society, and from some of the extremely primitivist instincts of early Greens we encountered in Chapter 4, by recognising that "almost all Greens are decentralist by inclination, but most support one variation or another of the 'both top-down *and* bottom up' model of government with grassroots initiatives given every opportunity to thrive through appropriate national legislation".[116]

In her book *Vulture Capitalism*, the Marxist writer Grace Blakeley exposes the reductive myth that the primary difference between the leftwing and the rightwing is that they favour big and small states, respectively.[117] This is too narrow a way of looking at things, and also simply incorrect. For a start, neoliberal states are big, interventionist states, ready to bail out banks and businesses with billions of pounds of the public's money. On the other side of the coin, there is also a long and proud history of Left traditions which have a more ambivalent relationship to the state, let alone a big one; such as the Left libertarians and anarchist tendencies which have animated the more radical wings of the Green Party membership through its history as recounted by Wall. Contrasted with the statist social democratic model of dominant traditions within the Labour Party, suspicion of the state in favour of decentralisation and autonomy might seem to echo with what figures like Scruton claim as conservatism, but is as much at home in socialist traditions which recognise that, for all the good it can do, the state is ultimately an instrument for upholding capitalism and empire.

This tendency was given articulation in the 1979 pamphlet *In and Against the State*, written by a collection of libertarian socialists called the London Edinburgh Weekend Return Group.[118] In it they argued that while socialists must wield state power and work within the public sector for the betterment of the working class, they must simultaneously work to subvert and transform it. Such a tradition was upheld by a historically significant wing of the Labour movement, most notably figureheaded by Tony Benn, and moreover put into real-life practice by figures like Ken Livingstone and John McDonnell on the Greater London Council (GLC) in the early 1980s. Opening the doors of County Hall to self-organised community groups like renters' unions and women's groups, the GLC actually shared power with Londoners and diverted real resources to community groups to be spent autonomously. Here we see the principles of decentralisation and democratisation not just championed by avowed and undeniable socialists but literally put into practice. Although rarely expressed in these terms, the GLC of the early 1980s arguably stands as one of the best examples of some of the defining principles of Green politics being given practical expression in the form of a lively, participatory and democratic municipal socialism. Thatcher, threatened by this counterpower, abolished it in 1985.

Ultimately, a marriage of Green philosophy and leftwing politics is only strictly necessary assuming you want to preserve a few things whose intrinsic virtues are usually assumed to go without saying: democracy, basic standards of living and the inherent dignity of all people. Should you be willing to discard such ideals, as are a frightening number of contemporary political figures, other futures are available. Put simply, there are plainly some extremely rightwing potential responses to conditions of planetary emergency. In *Climate Leviathan*, Joel Wainwright and Geoff Mann sketch out some possible political futures as we blast through average temperature records year on year. The titular model of a climate leviathan imagines capitalist sovereignty pooled at a planetary level. But they also imagine a business-as-usual scenario in which nation states try to maintain order in a predominantly capitalist global economy. The near-inevitable consequence of this will be a tendency towards authoritarianism, with worsening border violence and militarisation the response to the growing displacement, chaos and scarcity visited upon a sweltering earth.[119] The stirrings of such tendencies can be seen around the world today, with some of the growing support for far-right forces actively starting to take on the explicit language of eco-fascism.

One thing is for sure. The small-c conservative traditions which have hitherto had some legitimate claim on environmentalism in the forms of conservation and stewardship will be of less and less use to us in a hotter and hotter world untouched by political and economic transformation. Protecting pockets of nature or individual species will become an increasingly hopeless, Sisyphean battle as huge swathes of the planet become effectively uninhabitable and we descend further and further into a bona fide mass extinction event. The famous slogan of Rosa Luxemburg takes on added resonance as the twenty-first century wears on. We now choose between ecosocialism or eco-barbarism. Regrettably, the latter will happen by default, with the existing political order trying to preserve the privilege of an increasingly remote capitalist class for as long as can be maintained, while flames lick and dust billows around growing numbers of the wretched. Ecosocialism, by contrast, will have to be won through unprecedented struggle. Greens have rammed their fingertips into the crack of an emergency exit from the hell which awaits. Only an organised movement can kick that door open to discover what new world awaits on the other side.

6

Can the Greens Keep Winning Everywhere?

The day before launching the 2026 local elections campaign in Deptford, Zack Polanski made the last-minute decision to jump on a train to the seaside. On that afternoon of 8 April, he was heading to Margate in Kent for an emergency rally which had been called with less than 24 hours' notice in support of the Green candidate standing in a by-election the following day. Owing to the salience of immigration for communities across its coastline, Kent has long been a stronghold for Farage's various political vehicles. Never more so than during the present Reform surge. In the 2025 election, in which all seats for Kent County Council were being contested, Reform went from having absolutely no representation on the council to winning an astonishing 57 seats, giving them majority control of the council, overturning decades of Conservative rule.[120] A by-election was triggered and scheduled for 9 May, however, when a councillor in Margate was jailed after admitting controlling and coercive behaviour towards his wife.[121]

On paper you would not expect a Green to hold much hope of winning this seat. The disgraced Reform councillor had taken the ward with over 40 per cent of the vote less than a year prior to the by-election, while the Green candidate had come fourth with 12 per cent.[122] But when Polanski made it to the stone steps of the seafront, hundreds of people had gathered in support of the Green candidate: an offshore wind engineer named Rob Yates. Momentum was behind the Greens. The next morning, as residents of Margate took to polling stations, they returned Yates to the Council with 38.8 per cent of the vote.[123] "The Cliftonville win was hard fought for," Yates tells me.

> Persuading the public that we were the tactical anti-Reform vote and showing local achievements was critical in helping nudge the mood on the door from Green leaning to Green voting. Locally, we increased voter turnout, and took half of the Labour vote, and a small number of Tories. This proves that even in Reform strong areas, there is a majority – if you can get them voting – for a progressive left party.

The Reform vote was down. The Labour vote was down. The Conservative vote was down. The Greens were the beneficiaries and had decisively taken a scalp in the heart of what had become a Reform fortress. Polanski found himself on a train to the coast for the second time in three days, this time to celebrate a seismic victory. As he held Yates' arm aloft on the seafront of the Kent coast, with the sun sinking into the ocean behind them, the hundreds amassed watched another sunset on the stranglehold of the old party duopoly. The contours of English politics continued to crystallise into a contest between Greens and Reform. And on that day, the Greens proved that they could win in Farage heartlands.

The Greens' electoral base has traditionally been rooted in areas with two very different demographic compositions: taking seats in racially diverse inner-city areas populated with students, graduates and metropolitan leftwingers as well as in small-c conservative rural areas with older, upper-middle-class, predominantly white residents. Spun positively, this is presented as evidence that the Greens can win anywhere. Less charitably, this is also posed as a question of the extent to which this represents an outright contradiction by which the party will one day be undone. Polanski's leadership – in both its character and the step change it provided the Greens' electoral ambition – is poised to force the question. Some argued that Polanski's leadership, in its uncompromising appeal to its urban bases, would risk alienating its rural vote. As argued by Polanski's critics in the leadership election we explored in Chapter 2, only cautious, incremental gains spread between rural and urban areas could carry the Greens forward. But the victory in Margate – and the record-breaking gains across the country in the full local elections less than a month later – suggest otherwise. Polanski has held together the Greens' existing voting coalition while making significant electoral progress.

The 2024 general election provides a perfect case study of the Greens' split between two electoral bases. If you were to walk around North Herefordshire, for example, you would not exactly think of yourself as being in a place ripe with pre-revolutionary conditions. It's a rural seat dotted with market towns, overwhelmingly (if sparsely) populated by older people with relative economic security. The seat (or its closest equivalent prior to the 2010 boundary review) had been held by Conservatives since 1837, and the last time any opposing party had held the seat was when the Whigs won it in 1835. The incumbent MP Bill Wiggin had extended his majority in four successive general elections from 2010 to 2019 – in which he reached a high point of 63 per cent of the vote. But this is where, improbable as it may sound, Dr Ellie Chowns leapfrogged from fourth place to win the parliamentary seat for the Greens, advancing from just 9.3 per cent of the vote in 2019 to 43.2 per cent in 2024 – a swing of 34.4 per cent. This was to be the first time the Greens had ever won a parliamentary seat directly from the Tories.[124]

Adrian Ramsay pulled off a near identical feat in Waveney Valley – a very similar constituency on the border of Norfolk and Suffolk. Although technically a newly constituted seat in 2024 following the 2023 boundary review, comprised from parts of no less than five Conservative-held seats, Ramsay surpassed the projected 2019 result of an identical 9.3 per cent of the vote to achieve 41.7 per cent in the 2024 election, decisively beating the Conservatives into second place on just over 30 per cent.[125] The structural outcome of this pair of victories was to create a completely even split between the four Green parliamentary seats won (three of which for the first time) in the 2024 general election: Chowns and Ramsay representing rural seats in overwhelmingly conservative areas, while Carla Denyer took

Bristol Central, and Sian Berry retained Brighton Pavilion as a successor to Caroline Lucas. Both of these seats, by complete contrast, were inner city, won from Labour, and comprised of a more diverse, socially progressive and economically precarious electorate.

This split between urban and rural representation was a near perfect mirror of a split which had resulted from an absolute explosion of electoral success for the Green Party of England and Wales at the local level over the five years or so prior to this parliamentary breakthrough. The 2019 local elections saw the Greens double their representation in a single night, going from 179 councillors to 358, in part a legacy of the resources provided by the Green surge of 2015 described in Chapter 3.[126] The previous doubling, by contrast, had taken over a decade to achieve – going from 89 seats in 2006 to the 179 of 2018. Significant advances were made year on year from 2019, most notably in 2023 where the party broke another internal record by winning 481 seats in a single night.[127] Party members and activists were fond of sharing the resulting graph which charted the number of councillors representing the party: a near flat line almost imperceptibly sloping slightly upwards from the 1970s for decades on end before abruptly shooting upwards in 2019 as another near straight line with no apparent apex in sight.

The Greens had a watershed electoral year in 2019, not only with the doubling of councillors but also the shock result in the European elections mentioned in Chapter 3, winning 12 per cent of the vote and taking the number of Green MEPs from three to seven – including in their number Ellie Chowns. In the weeks and months following this result, as Brexit tensions continued at a rolling boil and the Greens provided a principled and radical vision for Remain, national polling kept the party hovering around an unprecedented high of 10 per cent.[128] But despite the resultant buoyancy among party membership, none of this was to translate into increased representation at the parliamentary level in the 2019 general election, where the Greens were again to be squeezed to just 2.6 per cent of the vote, as an electoral bloc once again rallied around Corbyn's Labour.[129] The deflation felt by many in the party was, to say the least, overshadowed by the broader trauma inflicted upon the wider Left when Johnson returned to Parliament a Conservative majority of 365. For some in the Greens, the fatalist thought took root that there was a hard ceiling on what the party could achieve at a national level. Perhaps Caroline Lucas' achievement in Brighton was a fluke that was never to be repeated.

Just five years later, the results of the 2024 election were to decisively confound these doubts, as Ramsay, Chowns, Berry and Denyer quadrupled the party's representation in the Commons. How was this achieved? For all of these seats (including Brighton when it was first won in 2010), this was the result of building upwards from an established base of councillors within the constituency. Undoubtedly, the quality of the candidates was a factor, to a person willing to put in the hard yards of grafting necessary to pull off such improbable electoral feats. Chowns and Ramsay in particular were certainly helped by the near unprecedented collapse in support for the outgoing Conservatives, who were swept away on a tide of resentment. While Labour were the natural beneficiaries of this almost everywhere, targeted campaigns supporting quasi-independent local candidates in the form of

Chowns and Ramsay had the ability to deliver breakthrough wins. All of this points to the single most important factor in the ability of the Greens to achieve this extraordinary step change in representation at both local and national level: an electoral campaigning technique known internally within the party as "target to win". This, above all else, is what can be credited with the Greens' justified reputation for being able to win seats from both Labour and Conservatives in both urban and rural areas.

For a three-word term which has become one of the most seminal, semi-controversial and certainly most often repeated within the active membership of the Green Party, it's not easy to provide a simple and universally agreed definition of what "target to win" actually means.

"I really hate the phrase 'target to win'", admits head of elections Chris Williams, explaining the process of how the Greens developed their electoral expertise over decades.

> All it originally meant was: the party needed to move away from the scattergun approach of saying nice things in the media and hoping a majority of people would notice and switch to voting Green. Clearly that wasn't a good strategy because people didn't hear about us in the media very much. Instead, we had to have a ruthless ground campaign where we create our own media through leaflets and one-to-one conversations and *lots* of listening and reflecting back what we can do about local issues.

Target to win, in a nutshell, is just focussing the resources you have (people and money) on the opportunities that you have.

This means taking a sober assessment of how many wards a given number of local volunteers and activists can realistically canvas on a weekly basis, allowing Greens to run hyperlocalised campaigns which speak to the genuine and pressing concerns of local residents, while the bigger parties often mindlessly shove mass-produced, identikit leaflets through the letterboxes of residents in safe seats or places they just aren't focussing on. This, irrespective of the political persuasion of local voters, puts Greens in a strong position to assert themselves as a committed local candidate in contrast to a complacent incumbent who has for too long taken their vote for granted – of which many such people can be found in both Labour and the Conservatives.

Some sort of strategy like this is necessary for a small party to make gains in a first-past-the-post electoral system, perhaps best evidenced on a macro level by the 2015 general election results in which the Greens quadrupled its vote relative to 2010 but failed to return any new parliamentarians alongside Caroline Lucas. Without concentrated support in specific seats, generalised rises in support are usually of little electoral consequence. This was the central insight behind the strategy of the 2024 general election in which just four seats were ruthlessly chosen, targeted and won. Incidentally, this formed one of the key fault lines in the leadership election of 2025, with Chowns and Ramsay arguing that their track record of successful deployment of "target to win" demonstrated an ability to win in difficult places. Conversely, Polanski's potential to raise the national polling numbers of the Greens was portrayed as being something of a glamour metric: an accolade which will impress the party faithful and make a buzz on social media but will not result in more Greens getting elected when that support is diffused non-strategically across the country or just piles up in places with existing Green MPs, pointlessly extending their majorities.

Given that Polanski never proposed throwing out targeted ground campaigns, the extent to which the leadership contest turned into a quasi-referendum on the notion of "target to win" was curious. Instead, his central pitch was that the Greens were being left behind on the national stage by a surging far right, and that Greens had a political obligation to step up to credibly oppose them, since Labour were manifestly failing to do so. Nevertheless, it is true to say that growing numbers of members – especially newer and younger members – are frustrated by the rigid and dogmatic application of "target to win" among longer-standing members who have internalised the methodology as a fixed process, rather than the evolving practice that Williams describes. "I've definitely seen situations where older members have had new members come in with fresh ideas and are met with an attitude of: no, we don't do that, we do 'target to win' and nothing must be changed," Williams tells me. "But if your electoral approach has fossilised so much that it doesn't work because the first time you used it was 15 years ago, and its edge is wearing because your approach hasn't been adapted … then there needs to be a new approach."

This is especially true when Polanski's leadership has delivered a step change in the key resources of people and funding, strengthening the hand of hungry new members who want to raise the horizons of the party's ambitions. Hau-Yu Tam, councillor in Lewisham, was told by figures in her local party in no uncertain terms that "we're never going to be able to expand beyond two target wards, so *do not* deviate from this strategy" as she recounts to me in early 2026. "Now we're in a space where, not without grief and tension, we have expanded the target wards and a whole host of development wards. With work and with patience and results, people do change their minds." To say the least, Tam was vindicated following the local elections of May 2026, when Lewisham went from four Greens (all a result of defections) to taking a breathtaking 40 seats, representing dominant control of the council with just 14 Labour councillors making up the opposition. They also won the mayoralty.[130]

The question of how the party balances electoral discipline with adaptability, experimentation and ambition is a question to which we will turn more fully in Chapter 7. But Michael Chessum, Green councillor in Lambeth, captures this tension in the membership when he argues that sometimes, rather than planning for elections two years away,

> we need to say: we're actually going to go out and talk about community issues. We're going to talk about big national issues. We are going to mobilise for a protest. We're gonna go and join a union. We're gonna get a strike going. And that is actually very much at odds with the prevailing culture of a lot of the Greens. For a lot of people who are attached to "target to win", it literally has not occurred to them that we might do that kind of work.

However this tension resolves itself, suffice to say for now that it is unlikely that Polanski's leadership will cause a complete erasure of institutional memory regarding how to win elections, despite that being raised as some sort of active fear during the leadership contest. "The party's electoral strategy is just a growing set of experiences, knowledge and tactics that, together, form a toolbox to enable people to win elections," Williams explains. "Skillsharing and adaptation is key. You need to be adaptable and continue to build on your previous learning. If you don't change, you get left behind."

No matter how the phrase is defined, and in spite of the practice sometimes being inflexibly applied, the positive impact of "target to win" to date cannot be understated: the Greens are now making huge advances in almost every election they stand in, and they have the ability in principle to win almost anywhere. The resultant electoral landscape of a nearly even split between conservative rural areas and progressive urban communities does, however, give rise to two tensions or challenges. The first is the question of whether this has been achieved by making directly contradictory appeals to urban and rural communities, and, if so, whether such a contradiction can endure when the Greens are contesting seats at greater scale. The second, more straightforwardly, is the claim that Polanski's communications style and political positioning will actively alienate people in rural areas. Do these accusations have merit and, if so, can these tensions be resolved?

If there is one wedge which political opponents most frequently attempt to drive between the urban and rural bases of the Greens, it's the accusation of NIMBYism among its rural voters, argued as being in contradiction to the interests of urban populations. NIMBYism (an acronym for the American-derived term "Not in my backyard") describes the phenomenon of people supporting the idea of something in the abstract – say, the building of council houses – but opposing it happening near to where they live. This accusation stalks the Greens in the countryside, where white, middle-class environmentalists are imagined to gleefully collude with the local council to put a stop to housebuilding, infrastructure and even clean energy projects. Amid the current Green surge, this has become a key attack line for Labour, going so far as to pull up a van outside the launch of the Greens' 2026 local elections campaign emblazoned with the claim that Greens had blocked 40,000 homes from being built. (Polanski, by reply, claimed that nobody could verify this number.)[131]

Back in 2024, within days of new Green MPs taking their seats in the Commons following the general election, the BBC ran the headline that Adrian Ramsay had called for a "pause on new pylons", a story which dominated the opening weeks of what should have been an exciting, insurgent new opening in UK politics.[132] A far more pernicious version of the NIMBY accusation descended upon the deputy leader Rachel Millward in rural Sussex in 2025, when she wrote a letter to the Home Office outlining her opposition to housing several hundred asylum seekers in a nearby army camp. This climaxed in a hostile public meeting in which a heaving room of angry residents bayed for Millward's resignation as council leader while protesters outside banged on the windows.[133] Other far-right pundits gleefully shared Millward's letter across social media, brandished as evidence of the fact that while young, urban Greens virtue signal about welcoming refugees, their councillors in small-c conservative areas say they don't want them there. The reality of Millward's position, lost in the narrative being woven by political opponents, was that she objected on the basis that it was inhumane for asylum seekers to be housed in an army camp and they should instead be integrated into communities properly, with a full right to work. This is a view shared, of course, by the so-called metropolitan idealists who enthusiastically returned Carla Denyer and Sian Berry to Parliament.

The rightwing targeting of Millward points to several defences against this accusation of NIMBYism. The first is that the claim is frequently weaponised in a dishonest way by political opponents. When Greens at local authority level object to housebuilding proposals, for example, it is often on the grounds that the developer has not included sufficient provision for social or affordable housing – and have instructed them to redraw the plans so that they are consistent with the local authority's targets. As the attack lines of opposing parties, this is rendered as straightforward, ideological opposition to housebuilding on behalf of a retiree class which wants to preserve the asset value of their property.

It's also only fair to concede that there are clearly things which people quite reasonably do not want in their backyard, such as incinerators and factory farms. Not only are such things inherently undesirable and environmentally destructive, but the negative externalities are often disproportionately absorbed by marginalised groups in society. Analysis from Friends of the Earth, for example, has found that racialised and low-income people are disproportionately concentrated in the 5 per cent of neighbourhoods still exposed to extreme air pollution.[134] At the same time, the benefits of such infrastructure are often big businesses and the richest in society, whether that be the developers turning could-be community assets into luxury flats or new aviation capacity being absorbed by a small number of high earners enjoying more and more holidays. Taking a principled opposition to infrastructure projects which combine environmental destruction with social injustice is an obvious plank of eco-populist politics.

All of this antagonism is being turbo charged by a nascent YIMBY movement, which, ironically, is providing the political platform for the Greens to unite their rural and urban voters in common interest. YIMBYs (a countervailing "Yes, in my backyard" movement) are a self-described group of people who are enthusiastically supportive of getting stuff built. This tendency has been bolstered by the 2025 book *Abundance*, by Ezra Klein and Derek Thompson, which they hoped would revive a moribund Democratic Party in the US by furnishing them with a political programme that promises to flood the economy with supply and revive the country with resulting economic growth.[135] In this regard, *Abundance* can be reduced to the sort of orthodox fetishisation of GDP which is anathema to Green politics. Anything which can be built must be built.

There is much to be sceptical about this way of looking at things. Firstly, it assumes a very uncomplicated model of supply and demand, assuming that the reason house prices are so high is purely because there aren't enough houses, and that to build more houses will bring down their price. Ditto with energy. This isn't really how the economy works, where high prices on life's essentials are rarely the result of absolute scarcity and are more commonly a problem of circulation and distribution. Secondly, if you turn on the taps of supply literally everywhere in the economy, when ecology demands that redistribution squashes aggregate consumption by constraining the wealthiest, the planet will be fried. In any event, in making this argument, the stakes for supporting new roads and runways are elevated from the relatively modest claims of making it easier to get around to a promise of national recovery and renewal. The formally parochial question of planning and development thus steps onto the stage of national politics.

This agenda has been imported to the UK, albeit characteristically translating the peppy and optimistic tone of the American movement to a distinctly British moan about form-filling and red tape. A burgeoning ecosystem of podcasts and think tanks has sprung up around the agenda (not without their links to known rightwing interests, such as the Looking For Growth group, which has been supported by Dominic Cummings).[136] Crucially, it has been adopted by the incumbent Labour government itself, most notably around the time, in January 2025, that they announced their intention to back the expansion of Heathrow Airport. Framed entirely around its capacity to drive economic growth (a claim convincingly undermined by analysis from the New Economics Foundation), this was the moment from which the prime minister and the Chancellor of the Exchequer lined up to make an active virtue of positioning themselves as antagonists to environmentalists.[137] Starmer set up a binary opposition between what he called the "builders" and the "blockers" while Reeves railed against the inhibiting effects of "bats and newts" on the timely delivery of infrastructural projects.[138] Never mind the fact that, as demonstrated by the Wildlife Trust, only 3 per cent of planning appeal decisions featured bats or newts as any sort of factor.[139] This was above all else a piece of political theatre, most vulgarly exemplified by the spectacle of Secretary of State Steve Reed attending Labour Party conference in a MAGA-aping hat, emblazoned with the slogan "build, baby, build". Still, this came with real political effects. A programme of unpicking the so-called red tape around planning (that is to say, removing environmental protections) followed. When this was spouted by then-chancellor Kwasi Kwarteng in the notorious so-called mini budget of 2022, this was widely and correctly perceived to be an aggressive free-market agenda of deregulation. Now this re-emerges as a salve to failing social democratic centrism.

From as far back as the 1980s, figures like Jonathon Porritt noted the downsides of Greens being associated with NIMBYism, warning of an "impulse to parochialism" resulting in Greens being "permanently on the defensive … instead of developing a critique of the way of life which leads to such threats".[140] Today there is an opening for the eco-populism of Polanski to knit together the conservationist instincts of the rural voter base with the more overt radicalism of younger, urban support in a more systemic way. The government's demonisation of citizens who care about nature in favour of corporate interest and abstract appeals to economic growth is the sort of political programme which can unite almost all wings of the Green Party in opposition. In the face of the erroneous assertion that covering the country in roads and runways will grow the economy, the Greens' long-standing analysis of such matters offers a compelling counterview: that the question of distribution within planetary limits must take precedence over the fantasy of endless growth. At a time when the Green Party is led by someone with the express political strategy of defining enemies and building coalitions of support along clear lines of antagonism, the incumbent government has willingly and deliberately set up the framework of such productive political conflict at the level of national politics. The result is the creation of common interest across bases of Green Party support previously assumed to be hopelessly divergent. NIMBYism can be reclaimed as anti-capitalism.

When it comes to the question of whether the political style of Polanski himself risks alienating Green support in small-c conservative seats, it's important to keep in mind that the distinction between rural and urban areas can be overemphasised, sometimes to the point of caricature. "I knocked on a lot of doors in North Herefordshire and Waverly Valley," Natalie Bennett tells me,

> and one of the things that's not adequately understood is that our voters in those places are not actually that different from our voters in other places. There are a lot of people concerned about the two-child benefit cap, child poverty and tuition fees in rural areas, just like there are in urban areas.

Too often, this issue is discussed as if Bristol and Brighton are populated entirely by vegans, and the countryside is populated solely by fox hunters. The reality is, of course, that there is a diversity of people who live in rural areas, including plenty of people from three constituencies key to the Green coalition.

The first is simply people who have generally socially and economically progressive views, aligned wholly with the core policy and political offer of the Green Party. Such people do live in villages. Indeed, beyond the electoral coalitions of the Greens specifically, there is a lot more alignment of views between urban and rural populations than the media framing of irreconcilable opposition would have you believe. A lot is made of the myth that the Greens must necessarily say one thing to urban voters and another set of things entirely to rural voters. But while it is obviously the case that, like any sophisticated contemporary political campaign, messaging is tailored to be targeted at specific audiences across the country, it's not the case that Greens are saying wholly incompatible things to different communities. While Chowns got on her waders to talk about the water quality in the River Wye, and Denyer called for an end to rip-off water costs for her squeezed constituents, the identified root cause and proposed policy response was the same: this was the product of the failure of the privatisation of water, which ought to be brought back into public ownership to clean up our waterways and bring down our bills. This analysis, packaged in eco-populist communications, has been used by Polanski to build a bridge between urban and rural voters on the national stage.

The second important constituency is the working class, which is again too often imagined to be confined to inner-city slums and poverty-stricken post-industrial towns. From farmers to call centre workers, here, too, are plenty of people who can in principle be organised along class lines. This is true in even the most pastoral locations of the UK. Many will be familiar with the process of enclosure from the twelfth century onwards, which consolidated and privatised large swathes of land, taking them out of the common stewardship of ordinary people and putting them into private hands for the purpose of profit accumulation. Less understood is the legacy of that process today. Guy Shrubsole, author of *Who Owns England?* and an activist with Right to Roam, draws attention to the fact that, today, half of England's land is owned by just 1 per cent of the population, with an estimated 92 per cent of England off limits to the public.[141] "I absolutely think that 'Middle England' is sceptical about the big landowners that own most of the countryside," he tells me, "but many folks remain either unaware of quite how much influence they still wield, or are understandably afraid of going up against powerful interests like the shooting lobby". The book *Rural*, by Rebecca Smith, chronicles some of these ongoing processes and experiences in living memory: workers dependent upon the natural world but subordinated to absentee landlords; farmers struggling to derive profit from a pint of milk; and near entire villages reduced to ghost towns by second homes and holiday lets.[142] The tentacles of capital reach into the countryside as much as they do into the city.

You can imagine building popular power across rural populations in resistance to such structural forces. Some pockets of rebellion already exist, such as the mass trespasses onto privately owned land organised by the likes of Right to Roam, most notably in the case of Dartmoor when multimillionaire hedge funder and landowner Alexander Darwall sought to upturn the status of the moor as the only place in England where one could camp without the landowner's permission. Hundreds of people participated in a mass trespass in 2023 in support of their continued right to access the land. In May 2025, the supreme court took the side of campaigners – finding that the right to wild camp on Dartmoor should be upheld.[143] There are further policy levers which could be pulled to remedy some of these issues. Most obviously is a right to freely roam the English countryside – something which already exists in Scotland and was promised by Labour ahead of the 2024 general election, though no word on it has been heard since their taking power. In addition, Scotland's version of community right to buy could also be imported: the right for a community group to register their interest in a piece of land or a building and to be first in the queue for purchasing it if the owner decides to sell. If the land or building is left abandoned and neglected, it can even trigger a compulsory purchase order. This is a mechanism which can play a part in keeping land and property in productive use for the community, rather than ending up in the hands of profit-seeking developers. Campaigns for such policies could form the basis of radical, agitational, class-based politics in the countryside.

Poverty is also rife. The idyll of the countryside is often imagined to be the preserve of the middle class and rich who have elbowed lower earners out of the scarce supply of housing stock, and, indeed, while poverty rates are *slightly* lower than urban areas, approximately 1.6 million people were nonetheless experiencing poverty in rural England in 2020.[144] As in cities, the people displaced by this gentrification-like process still have to go somewhere. Fuel poverty in particular is actually higher than in urban areas, on account of the greater dependency of people using oil burners.[145] Under present conditions of fossil fuel volatility owing to the atrocities unfolding in the Middle East, such pressures are only likely to grow. Related to all this is the third group of note: a middle class being consciously reabsorbed into the 99 per cent – either through the direct experience of downward social mobility and a squeeze in living standards or through being forced to see their children priced out of the place they grew up in or unable to leave the family home at all. As Polanski repeated frequently through the leadership campaign, inequality hurts you wherever you live. That includes rural voters who share both the values and the material interests of the people who vote Green in Bristol and Brighton.

The first major stress test of Polanski being able to bridge his urban and rural bases came in May 2026, when local elections took place all over England. As might be expected, the headline gains came in the former Labour heartland of London, where Greens swept to power in Hackney, Lewisham and – most astonishingly – Waltham Forest where they went from having no Greens on the council to winning an outright majority with 31 seats – the biggest ever breakthrough onto a council in Green Party history. All of this points to the sort of gains which were expected to be achieved under a Polanski leadership that appealed to inner-city populations repulsed by an atrophying Labour Party.

The feared reversal of fortunes in rural places, however, largely failed to occur. In both Norfolk and Suffolk – the areas across which Adrian Ramsay's previously Conservative parliamentary seat is split – Greens went forward, gaining eight seats in Norfolk to secure a total of 12, and gaining four seats in Suffolk to secure a total of 13. These seats were taken from a mixture of Labour, Tories and even a Lib Dem. In West Sussex, half a dozen gains – including two from Reform seats – took the Greens from one councillor to seven. Eleven gains were made in the East Sussex elections, despite this being one of the elections which was subject to being cancelled but suddenly reinstated. Eight gains were taken in the largely Conservative East Surrey. The list goes on.

Perhaps even more noteworthy than these gains made across largely Conservative rural councils such as the above would be the examples of wins which don't quite fit into either of the archetypal camps of the Greens' two electoral bases. Consider Hastings. This is a coastal town with no university which voted for Brexit and returned Conservative MPs to Parliament in general elections from 2010 until 2024 (on three occasions the former home secretary Amber Rudd). It's neither the multiracial, graduate-centric metropolis of Bristol Central nor the white, upper-middle class, retiree-centric leafy enclave of Hereford North. Yet in May 2026, Greens gained one more councillor than Reform to take overall control of the council. Results like this transcend the urban–rural dichotomy previously applied to the Greens.

The local election results suggest that Polanski's leadership is shaking off the perception of the Greens as the preserve of the white middle class, and further establishing the party as being rooted in an electorate of racially diverse, economically deprived communities – as evidenced by paper candidates in the poorest parts of a place like Haringey leaving their rival Labour candidates for dust. At the same time, this was achieved without meaningfully alienating the existing support Greens have in leafy, suburban and rural areas – indeed, in many such areas, they advanced. Many previously assumed these outcomes to be mutually exclusive. A glimpse of this electoral prize was granted when Rob Yates' hand was raised in victory on the beach of Margate in April 2026. A month later the point was proven emphatically: the Greens can still win everywhere.

7

Are Elections the Only Thing That Matters?

Extinction Rebellion roared into life in November 2018 with a demonstration of its ability to mobilise huge numbers of people in service of ambitious and risky direct action. Five of the most well-used bridges in central London were brought to a standstill by thousands of activists calling for action on the climate emergency. Zack Polanski, addressing an assembled crowd with a megaphone, was one of dozens led away in handcuffs that day.[146]

Polanski is among several high-profile Greens to be arrested for peaceful civil disobedience. Caroline Lucas was arrested in 2013 during a protest against fracking while her future co-leader Jonathan Bartley went on to be arrested in late 2019 in defiance of the Section 14 powers used to prohibit peaceful Extinction Rebellion actions.[147] A month later, Ellie Chowns (then MEP) met the same fate when joining an assembly on Trafalgar Square.[148]

Of course, throwing yourself to the mercy of the criminal justice system is nothing to fetishise, not least when those arrested are white people in positions of relative economic and social privilege. But these anecdotes do speak to the genuine conviction within Greens to both support and actively participate in wider social movements outside of electoral cycles.

To be clear, the Green Party of England and Wales is first and foremost an electoral project. Despite the anti-statist and anarchistic tendencies within the membership described by Derek Wall in Chapter 5, and the growing hegemony of ecosocialism within the party, there are no notable revolutionary tendencies within the Greens. It is fundamentally a reformist party (that is to say, it seeks to deliver change through conventional democratic means) within which the typical member would completely take for granted that Green candidates winning elections is the main purpose of the party. That said, some of the tensions outlined in Chapter 6 regarding some members' protectiveness of the "target to win" strategy stem from concern that fellow members are deviating too much from electoralism and are instead more drawn to direct action, community organising and issues-based campaigning. For such people, the explicit purpose of the foundation of the Green Party was to be distinct from social movements and campaigners, sometimes referring to themselves as "the political wing of the environmental movement". The *raison d'être* of the party was to win and wield state power.

Polanski's leadership campaign, however, leaned into the tendency within the party more drawn to broader political activity, arguing that social movements could and should be harnessed and channelled towards the broader consolidation of power on the Left. "I think we're at our best when we organise with local communities," Polanski tells me. "When we campaign on an issue as a candidate, and then get elected to *continue* to campaign on the issue – and ideally resolve it." This vision of a party which acts as a locus point for a host of tributary movements and wider Left institutions is a compelling one. It may also be necessary if the Greens are to have any chance of actually implementing anything close to an ecosocialist programme should they win state power. The sobering strategic question is: can it be achieved under present social and political conditions? And, if so, can Zack Polanski and the Greens be the ones to do it?

The 2010s was a decade characterised by surges of Left optimism, albeit hopelessly shackled to a pendulum swinging between electoralism and movement building. As we saw in Chapter 3, the 2008 economic crisis gave way to a wave of resurgent street protest in the UK, in opposition to a Conservative agenda of austerity and marketisation, which began to bite from their ascension to power in 2010. This resurgence of such politicisation was not restricted to the UK. Across much of the world, similar movements sprung from the resentment of crushed populations expected to pay for the greed of reckless speculators through the devastation of public services and spaces. In the US, this took the form of Occupy Wall Street, while across mainland Europe the so-called "Movement of the Squares" saw tens of thousands of people reclaiming public spaces. Wherever they appeared, these movements and moments shared a few key characteristics. Firstly, this was the initial conception of the 99 per cent, in which popular class solidarity among the vast majority of populations was enjoined in opposition to a vanishingly small number of people who had enriched themselves by ruining the lives of millions. Secondly, these movements were notable for being deliberately leaderless and non-hierarchical, in what is often termed to be a "horizontalist" formation, that is, a quasi-anarchic structure whereby decisions are made by consensus in open assemblies in which anyone can participate. Admirable for their commitment to utopian horizons of democratic ideals, these movements were ultimately to be unsuccessful in their primary aims. In none of these countries was a progressive programme of Keynesian economic stimulation delivered to recover from the financial crash in a way which would have invested in the public realm and the green transition. Instead, we were, almost to a country, visited by the pain of austerity.

By the middle of the decade, a notable pivot to electoralism had occurred; these popular movements giving way to shock advancements for insurgent Left and anti-establishment candidates as social democratic centrist parties went into freefall with no answers to the economic conundrums posed by the 2008 crisis. In the UK, that looked like Jeremy Corbyn winning the Labour leadership in a landslide, to the shock of almost everyone, including himself. In the US, Bernie Sanders came closer than anyone would ever have expected to becoming the Democratic candidate in 2016, thwarted perhaps only by the uniquely high barriers of entry to insurgent candidates in the US presidential system (not least the barrier of the Democratic Party itself). In Europe, the far-left party Podemos won over 20 per cent of the vote and became the third-biggest party of parliament in Spain, just one year after being formed, while the democratic socialist party Syriza actually formed a coalition government in 2015. Here again, though, all of these electoral ambitions were to be thwarted, either by failing to seize state power or by being crushed and co-opted by greater political forces. The most notorious example of this would be Syriza, who were elected on an anti-austerity platform only to be reduced to the humiliation of capitulating to the EU and administering the austerity to which they were opposed.[149]

Two considerations arise from this cycle of Left disappointment through the 2010s. The first is how we can escape the oscillation between short-term electoralism and longer-term movement politics and find a way of synthesising these priorities and time horizons. The second is how we can ensure that electoral gains can be translated into real political transformation that changes people's lives. Both of these questions, as we will see, are entwined.

Professor of cultural and political theory Jeremy Gilbert has long made the persuasive case that there is no prospect of a leftwing regime enacting a radical anti-capitalist programme in government if it were not supported and defended by an outright majority of the population. Without it, the countervailing forces of capital – with all of its aligned institutional powers in the state, media and finance – would crush such a government, as we saw in the scattered examples of Left electoral success in the 2010s. In his excellent chronicle of the UK Left in the 2010s, Michael Chessum argues that one of the primary features of Corbynism's failure was its inability to root the project in a social base, having been battered by the whiplash pace of subordinating members to the immediate demands of snap general elections and internal conflict.[150] Figures close to Corbyn, such as Labour's then director of strategic communications James Schneider, subsequently reported a strain of naivety among others in the team who appeared to hold the belief that socialist reforms could be delivered by simply forming a government and enacting the policies of the manifesto, and anticipated none of this being frustrated by other arms of the state or global capitalist forces.[151]

Accusations of similar naivety can be levelled at the Greens in general. For a lot of their history, Greens have operated as if politics were merely a marketplace of ideas, in which the best ones will eventually win out. Less prominent has been a robust analysis of how political power is actually built and exerted. As Richard Seymour has put it: "one reason why it simply isn't good enough to 'win the battle of ideas' is precisely that people take far too much pleasure in their beliefs to give them up for a well-articulated policy statement".[152] The Greens' recent evolution into a more formidable electoral force has demonstrated an understanding that hundreds of thousands of words of good policy are worth very little if you don't hold power. Still, today the Green analysis of state power is largely limited to simply believing that electing Greens is preferable to electing candidates from other parties. A common electioneering slogan for candidates seeking to break onto a council was to appeal to the value of having "a Green in the room" – a fair appeal as far as it went. But as the Green Party surges under Polanski, and hovers over the possibility of becoming the primary party of the Left in England, a further stage of evolution is now required to equip incoming Greens with the imagination and tools to deal with the immensely complex practicalities and politics of delivering radical leftwing programmes from Green-led regimes. The most obvious working example of this is how Green councils can overcome the problem of local authorities being stripped of funding and left to implement austerity at a local level whether they like it or not. Ahead of the May 2026 elections, scores of Green candidates pledged to oppose austerity if they were elected.[153] Having gained five councils in those elections, how they will actually do this in practical terms is a different question entirely. Any good answer to that question will require a strong social base.

Polanski's political base within the party, such as the leading figures among GO, has a more clear-sighted understanding of the relationships between social forces and state power. As such, they have more strongly emphasised the strategic need for community organising and movement building as something that is directly complementary to, rather than a distraction from, electoralism. On this front, the most commonly cited working example from the actually existing Left at the moment is the Workers' Party of Belgium, a Marxist party which explicitly employs community-organising methods to build class solidarity and power across society. One of their units of organising is the "base group" – a small group of people concentrated in a physical location, conducting surveys and listening exercises with local residents to discover their actual needs and concerns. Such groups are then the basis of campaigning for tangible wins in the community, like keeping open a local swimming pool or library. One of the most notable manifestations of this organising is Medicine for the People – a network of free, community health centres in working-class areas. Furthermore, as well as treating the symptoms of poor health, they organise to tackle the root causes too, such as higher air pollution in areas of deeper deprivation. Such practices have deep roots in history. Consider the Black Panthers – a Black socialist organisation from the 1960s – who ran what were called "survival programmes": self-organised networks of people providing free groceries, free breakfast for kids and free medical aid, to protect their racialised class from the poverty to which they were being subjected. The Workers' Party of Belgium is today a contemporary example of enacting this key political principle: listening to the material needs of the community and attending to them. In the 2024 elections, the Workers' Party of Belgium advanced almost everywhere.[154]

This model of movement building and community organising is naturally complementary to the Greens in several key respects. The first and most obvious is that – as we saw in Chapter 6 – this is basically how Greens win elections anyway: running hyperlocal campaigns which listen to local residents and are responsive to their actual concerns. It also chimes strongly with the party's strong tendencies towards decentralisation, localism and mild suspicion of the state. Put simply, Greens are great believers in rolling up your sleeves and getting on with things, rather than waiting for the state to step in – especially when it might never do so. An example of this was on display in a viral video posted by Hannah Spencer before she was elected to Parliament.[155] Pointing to the many Union Jacks which had been mounted on rows of lampposts, she acknowledged the great effort and skill which would have been required to actually get those flags up there, and called upon the people responsible to put those practical skills to more productive use in the community: clear-ups, gardening clubs, fixing broken fencing. Often, this impulse within Greens is not expressly politicised and is instead the natural expression of the values of caring, community-minded people. Under Polanski, however, this could be formalised as community-organising units and understood in the more conventionally Marxist sense of base building, in which such networks and organisations are constructed as self-conscious alternatives to capitalist institutions. In short, Greens could learn the positive lessons of the Workers' Party of Belgium.

Polanski himself favours a porousness between Greens and local community campaigns and social movements. "I think this kind of fluidity is exactly where I want the party to be," he says.

> I've always been sceptical about community organising being entirely within the Green Party brand, because I think you get to a point where you organise, you get people elected, and then the organising stops because the organiser's been elected. I think it's healthy to have people who are sympathetic to the aims of the party, and indeed might be in the party, but where the organising is a separate function to the party. This helps ensure people elected by the party can be held accountable by the same organiser.

In recent years, the mutual aid networks developed during the Covid emergency were a perfect expression of this sort of Green politics in action, where self-organised units of ordinary neighbours pulled together to form safety nets for everyone in their locality, street by street. This phrase "mutual aid" was derived from a set of essays published in the early 1900s by the anarchist Peter Kropotkin. In this tradition, the principle of solidarity usurps the principle of charity: the people giving and receiving aid are equals to one another, rather than a paternalistic benefactor and passive beneficiary. This appeals to core Green political values: the recognition of our interdependence with one another, in direct contradiction to the dominant neoliberal claim that we are all individuals engaged in constant competition. The principles of mutual aid root a nonstate politics in the values of care and collectivity.

Greens also understand that stronger community resilience will be required to endure the climate impacts (and the attendant social, economic and political shocks which will accompany them) of the decades ahead. As Adam Greenfield puts it, the "long emergency" of the climate crisis means that "we will be compelled to take on a much greater share of the responsibility of caring for ourselves than most of us are accustomed to, as individuals and communities both".[156] In his book *Lifehouse*, he uses the case study of the self-organised mutual aid networks of citizens in the aftermath of Hurricane Sandy in New York to sketch out a vision for a future in which everyone has access to a "lifehouse" within a few streets of wherever they live, providing food, energy and shelter for anyone who needs it owing to the "depredations of neoliberal austerity *now*, as well as the storms to come".[157] Could local Green Party branches create similar resources within their communities? Such forms of collective organising which challenge the atomisation and individualism into which we have become imprisoned will be pivotal to enduring the challenges of the years ahead, while also building the social conditions for a likelier transition to decentralised ecosocialism. "Any sufficiently dense network of communities self-managed in this way," Greenfield argues, "begins to look like the first subtle stirrings of a nonstate society, organised from the bottom up."[158]

Before we lose ourselves too deeply in dreams of nonstate politics, however, we are compelled to return to the point that the Green Party is ultimately an electoral project. And so we turn to the question: what do we expect Greens to do once elected? There is little point in assembling the social conditions for delivering a transformational political programme if there is no strategy for wielding state power. Clearly, Greens are a significant electoral force in the UK today. But given that the current support for Greens – and socialism – sits within a significant but ultimately minority proportion of the public, elected Greens will be forced to grapple with one or more of three tricky problems: assuming power in extremely challenging circumstances; finding themselves a junior partner in power-sharing situations; and, perhaps, needing to negotiate electoral pacts to win power. How ought all this to be navigated?

Briefly putting aside the question of constructing a social base – a project which may take generations – we are confronted with the much more immediate concern of how a slew of newly elected Green councils ought to actually administer state power. It's a nice problem to have. But the Greens who swept into power in the May 2026 elections teeter on a tightrope between two sheer drops. On one side is outright failure: being completely overwhelmed by the task which stands before them and political inexperience resulting in them being chewed up and spat out by structural problems and antagonistic forces. On the other side is political failure: failing to set their sights beyond the ambition of managing and administering the crises in which they find their local authority and simply doing their best to make cuts in the fairest and least painful ways possible. Rather than tumbling into either abyss, the Greens must keep their balance and walk the tightrope towards a horizon of more transformational politics.

This will not be easy. The most frequently cited historical precedent for leftwing-controlled local authorities seeking to resist cuts from central government was the wave of Labour-led councils in the late 1970s and early 1980s who, rather than accept the restrictions on spending mandated by central government, refused to set any budget at all. While a tenacious campaign, it ultimately failed. Some of the councillors who held out longest were forced to repay losses to the council and were barred from standing for office. Subsequent legislation from the Conservative government (most notably the Rates Act 1984) would make the campaign even harder to repeat today. Still, some figures on the hard left cling to the tactic, such as members of Your Party who successfully passed a "no cuts" budget motion at its founding conference. Yet even when Jeremy Corbyn was Labour leader he advised against setting illegal budgets on the grounds that it would be utterly self-defeating.[159] If Greens set an unbalanced, illegal anti-austerity budget today, the result would be that they would all be thrown out of office, commissioners would come in and make the cuts without any consideration for questions of equity, local members would be demoralised, and a bunch of councillors from another party would likely take their place. Nothing about this would be desirable. To do this sporadically in a handful of easily isolated Green councils would be a disaster.

What then is to be done? A crucial piece of the puzzle will be to build collective power. Within the GO anti-austerity pledge signed by 200 Green councillors and candidates was a commitment to organising an emergency summit of all willing councillors (and MPs, community groups and trade unions) to plan and coordinate a national cross-party campaign to restore proper local authority funding. This could exert significant political pressure and extract concessions from a Labour government. In the meantime, Green councils will also have to think creatively about how they can empower local residents and address material concerns under present constraints. The history of the Greater London Council, referenced in Chapter 5, will likely act as a good historical guide for ways in which power and resources, such as they are, can be distributed through the local community. Tactics and practices like participatory budgeting (allowing residents to actually democratically control local spending) and local assemblies will play a role. Brand new thinking will also be necessary. In Haringey, the local party has worked with the leftwing think tank Abundance (not to be confused with the Abundance movement described in Chapter 6) to work up practical plans for implementing something called a "Popular Asset Commission" which would exist to allow the community to take ownership over assets, and then exert democratic control over the surplus they produce.[160] Most notably, this is a means of taking seriously the *transition* to ecosocialism, starting from the actually existing circumstances in which we find ourselves. Now that Greens are the biggest party on Haringey council, this work can begin.

At the national level, there is little prospect of Greens forming a majority government in 2029. A more likely upper ambition is the prospect of winning enough seats to hold the balance of power, or to be a junior partner in a coalition, whether formal or informal. But to ensure that this happens – as opposed to the Greens finding themselves as an appendage of MPs among opposition to a Farage-led government – will likely require electoral coordination of some kind. Caroline Lucas has long been a foremost advocate for this more collaborative and pluralist approach to politics, calling for (on one occasion as an editor of a book) a so-called progressive alliance, the logic of which runs something like this: opinion polling consistently shows majoritarian support for left-of-centre politics in the UK, but the distortion of the first-past-the-post election system means we keep ending up with Conservative-led governments which most of us didn't want. To remedy this, progressive parties should reach agreements to stand one representative candidate between them, based on who has the best shot of winning balanced with what is considered to be fair in aggregate at a national level.[161] Once elected, this government brings in proportional representation and the exercise need never be repeated.

Others agree with Lucas' analysis. Jeremy Gilbert has long posed the challenge to non-pluralists of the Left: how do you transcend the problem of the apparent ceiling of support for socialism at about a third of the country? Large enough to demand political representation, it is nonetheless not a big enough constituency to, by itself, win state power through elections. For such people, cross-party coalitions are an unavoidable aspect of delivering any form of transformational programme.

Soon after Polanski became leader, former Green Party co-leader Jonathan Bartley appeared on a Compass podcast, restating his belief that, had Corbyn not slammed the door in the face of the Greens in 2017, a Labour-led government would likely have been formed.[162] Obviously it is not possible to prove such a claim about a hypothetical alternative history. But we do know that the Labourist insistence on going for broke under first past the post came up short.

Still, some people cling to this hope that the distortions of first past the post can be harnessed to return a parliamentary majority without commanding a majority in the country. In fairness, this is precisely what gave rise to the present government: a distribution of votes which resulted in a nosebleed-inducing majority in the Commons on the basis of a historically low popular vote in the country. The justified contempt for Keir Starmer and his closest aid, Morgan McSweeney, can obscure the strategic success of what was achieved in the 2024 election in this regard, often dismissively attributed to dumb luck and the byproduct of the utter collapse of Tory support. It is, however, at least in part an instructive lesson of how first past the post can be manipulated. Had Starmer and his government had any vision for what they wanted to achieve with state power, a great deal of good could have been done with their result in the 2024 election. For Greens, of course, there is presently very little prospect of their level of support being distributed in such a way that a parliamentary majority is achieved.

Polanski ruled out any sort of national level coordination with Labour under Starmer. It is safe to say this would remain the case for any prospective successor to his right. Assuming that a soft-left candidate like Andy Burnham is prime minister heading into the next election, the pressure from members of both parties to negotiate some sort of arrangement which denies Reform a working majority will be immense. Should he choose to do so, Polanski will enter into such negotiations in a position of much greater strength than the Greens have ever enjoyed. Furthermore, in a figure like Burnham, Greens would be negotiating with someone who has previously been openly favourable towards electoral reform and, by extension and implication, a more pluralist politics.[163] This might help further open the door to cooperation.

On the other hand, there will be two countervailing forces. Firstly, there will be pressure upon any Labour leader who has even modestly reversed Labour's polling crisis to go for broke, squeeze the Greens and try to win big once again under first past the post. Secondly, there is the more entrenched feeling within a significant segment of the Green membership that, owing to the experience of standing aside for Labour in many seats in 2017 with absolutely nothing to show for it (not even acknowledgement), there is little appetite to do so again, least of all for a leader running on a much less radical prospectus. Such feelings are entirely justified. But the result might be a re-run of the 2017 general election. This time, that would mean Nigel Farage as prime minister.

Let us assume (and hope) that some combination of national leadership, local coordination and tactical voting returns to Parliament a semi-progressive government within which Greens are playing either a formal role or hold the balance of power. After breathing a justified sigh of relief, Greens would, yet again, find themselves in a perilous situation. History is littered with junior coalition partners who have been co-opted, compromised and chewed up by prevailing establishment forces. Again, in the scheme of Green Party history, these are good problems to have. But Polanski will nonetheless need to enter into any such Parliament with an extremely robust strategy and a clear sense of what concessions he will insist on extracting. Wisely, he will not be drawn on this question so far out from an election, focussing instead on maximising the Green vote rather than feeding speculation about parliamentary horse-trading. One can reasonably assume, though, given his political background, his own stated priorities and the obvious strategic logic to doing so, electoral reform is likely to be a key point of negotiation. If this were to be established, the vision underpinning Lucas' progressive alliance would finally be realised. Never again could Greens be punished by the distortions of first past the post.

Beyond sharp strategy at the top, two further things are required to ensure that a Green bloc wielding parliamentary power is not crushed by bigger political forces: a core base to push the elected Greens further and hold them to account and a wider majoritarian movement of support to enable (and defend) whatever ecosocialist reforms are implemented. We return then, full circle, to the necessity of a strong social base. As Michael Chessum puts it:

> If we see off Reform by propping up a Labour government that is crap, all that means is that we get Reform later down the line and worse. And then we're the 2020s Lib Dems. What we need to do is prepare to win electorally, but the most

> important thing is that this political force becomes a social force. That for me is the million-dollar question. How do we enact that?

In Anton Jager's *Hyperpolitics*, he argues that, while we live in an era in which people have never been so politicised, nothing seems to change. He attributes this to the lack of institutional form to support political activity.[164] Black Lives Matter mobilised nearly a tenth of adult Americans – easily the largest wave of protest of its kind. But without being rooted in institutions, such as political parties, unions or religious groups, these moments of mobilisation burn out as quickly as they burst into life. Over the period of neoliberal politics, civic life and participation has been deliberately hollowed out. Union density and militancy have collapsed. Churches have emptied. Political party membership – with some notable exceptions and spikes – has fallen sharply. Interestingly, the rise of Green parties across the world has coincided with the era of the decline of nineteenth- and twentieth-century mass politics.

As Greens formed parties from the early 1970s, the atomisation of society soon after began in earnest, and the dominant institutional form of civic society flipped from being the trade union to the NGO. Critically, this is a switch from mass-membership models to small groups of professionals. The Greens have never known a society of mass politics and high political education. As such, the lack of a culture of active political participation is arguably one of the obvious weaknesses of the Greens' history and current position (although, in fairness, it is not a problem which is unique to the Greens).

This weakness is perhaps best evidenced by the party's extremely low turnouts for internal elections, betraying a culture of passivity among the membership which can be inclined towards seeing their monthly financial payment as the full extent of their contribution to the organisation's success. In this regard, the Greens' membership structure shares characteristics with the broader norms of the era of NGOs, where membership connotes alignment with the aims and values of the organisation and members hand over money for the organisation to just crack on and do good stuff. This stands in contrast to how a figure like Jeremy Gilbert justifies his continued membership of Labour: which is to note that political parties are not like, for example, the Woodland Trust, where you become a member because you admire the work of the Woodland Trust. They are instead themselves terrains of political struggle which require the active and democratic participation of members to shape consensus and build power. You do not have to like a party leader to recognise the political utility of the democratic institution they oversee and the value of being a member which can shape that institution.

Changing this culture is key to resolving the apparently conflicting priorities of electoralism and movement building. "The problem with this dual strategy," writes Keir Milburn, "is that electoral politics has strong tendencies towards demobilising and eliding all other modes of politics. It imposes its own temporality of electoral cycles which don't fit the temporality of movements."[165] There is undoubtedly at least some tension between the short-term imperatives of electoralism and long-term horizons of building lasting political power, as evidenced by the fruitless oscillations of the 2010s. As Richard Seymour noted during the Corbyn leadership, "ideological territories are shaped over generations, not in time for electoral cycles. But electoral cycles will not wait for Corbyn's long game."[166] Nor so for the Greens. While the Greens have in recent years become expert at delivering a ground game which has delivered immediate electoral success, this has arguably come at the expense of a culture which cultivates high ideological coherence among its members and the ability to broaden their base within the wider public. Can Polanski shift the party culture to one of lively and active political participation?

Polanski's positioning of the Greens as a party that can attract much wider support is a good starting point, harking back to the days of mass politics. In 2026, 230,000 members seems like a lot to the Greens – and it undoubtedly is relative to the party's own past and the contemporary norms for mainstream parties across the West today – but pales in comparison to what was fairly routine a century ago. In the early 1950s, the Conservative Party had nearly 3 million members.[167] It is now becoming widely recognised on the Left of politics that rebuilding a culture of mass politics and political education will be a key prerequisite of building the power needed to deliver transformative policies which can truly challenge the hegemony of capital. As Jager puts it, "without a reinstitutionalisation of political engagement, the left will remain hostage to impotent vitality, and its adversaries will continue to enjoy a decisive advantage".[168] A mass-membership Green Party could be part of the escape from the oscillation between movement building and electoralism which drove the left into so many dead ends during the preceding decade.

In the end, the breakwater between winning elections and

building broader political power will have to dissolve. Such a distinction only really makes sense in the context of seeking to win handfuls of seats in spurts of incremental progress. With horizons lifted to the reality of actually holding state power at the local level, and the possibility of holding it at national level, the question of the social conditions in which such Green regimes will find themselves becomes much more pertinent. In this regard, the two imperatives are necessarily interlocked. Movement building, political education and class formation *are* electoralism. That said, there is still a meaningful distinction to be drawn on the question of the primary goal of the Green Party and the time horizon which would be attendant upon it. For the Marxist left, and for many still associated with Your Party, there is a project which spans generations of reconstituting the working class as a class for itself. This is not the primary aim of the Green Party, and while it could and should play a part in realising this goal, it is ultimately the collective responsibility of the wider Left, in an ecosystem of fluidity which Polanski describes. The animating purpose of the Green Party of England and Wales, then, will always be to form the first ever Green government. And while still improbable, it has never felt more possible than it has today.

8

Do the Greens Still Care about the Environment?

"What about *the environment?*" complained former Liberal Democrat adviser Polly Mackenzie on Times Radio the month after Zack Polanski won the leadership. "I really hate that the Green Party is not really very Green!"

"I think it's a secondary consideration," Daniel Finkelstein replied by way of agreement. "He never talks about it!"[169] This has been one of the commonest accusations levelled against Polanski since becoming leader of the Green Party of England and Wales: that he has junked the traditionally central concern of the environment in favour of a broad, leftwing economic populism. But does the accusation contain any merit? And would it matter if it did?

First of all, contrary to what Lord Finkelstein claims, it's simply not true to say that Polanski never talks about the environment, as can be seen through his time as a London Assembly member, pushing the mayor of London on retrofitting, aviation expansion and climate assemblies. Nevertheless, we can concede that he has de-emphasised an explicitly environmentalist framing in service of foregrounding a broader suite of social and economic concerns. The strategic reasons for this are threefold. Firstly, voters already overwhelmingly associate the Greens with the environment, with 34 per cent of the public saying that the Greens are the party they trust most on the environment, and the next closest party (Reform, interestingly) in a distant second on 10 per cent. Out of 18 policy areas polled, this was the highest level of trust recorded for *any party on any issue*. The Greens are more trusted on the environment than Reform is trusted on immigration.[170] This territory is decisively owned by the Greens to a degree that has no obvious parallel in modern politics.

Secondly, there is a blunt political reality that the cost-of-living crisis has absolutely and understandably dominated the electorate's topmost concerns for several years, and any insurgent political project which seeks to have mass appeal is going to need to address this – rather than shouting louder about a policy area which is falling in salience for a growing number of voters. Of the small number of people who are politically motivated by the environment alone, the vast majority are already voting Green.

Thirdly, Green Party members are completely alive to the above facts and have longed for a leader who can successfully break the party out of the straitjacket in which the establishment media is desperate to imprison them. Polling from August 2025 (notably before the explosion of new members from September

2025) found that members overwhelmingly backed the party expanding its focus. An astonishing 91 per cent of members agreed that "it's important for the Green Party to offer a wide range of policies covering a range of different issues". Just 3 per cent agreed, conversely, with the proposition that "The Green Party must focus its time and resources on the environment and campaigning against climate change."[171]

This need not surprise us. The reality is that, as Greens have always said, there should be no meaningful distinction between people and planet in a political philosophy which enables both to thrive. In their 1988 book *The Coming of the Greens*, Jonathon Porritt and David Winner go so far as to draw a specific distinction between the Green movement and the environmental movement, characterising the latter as "those people who believe that dying forests, polluted lakes, nuclear power stations and the clubbing of baby seals are 'A Bad Thing' – but who do not necessarily go on to conclude that it is therefore necessary to change the whole basis on which society is organised".[172]

This is a point of distinction with a political establishment which clings to the fantasy that our overlapping environmental crises can be tackled while carrying on with business as usual. Or that it can be siphoned off from other political issues and tackled in isolation. A case in point is provided by that same Polly Mackenzie who infamously once proudly tweeted that, during the Coalition government, the Liberal Democrats were able to extract a five-pence surcharge on disposable carrier bags from the Conservatives in return for Lib Dem support on tightening welfare sanctions. There are few more vulgar examples of a mindset which believes environmental solutions can be siloed from wider social and economic policy. Contrary to her complaint, it's politics like this which are, in her words, "not really very Green".

If there is anything which demands a collective political response, a break from market logic, and a direct challenge to capitalism, it's the climate crisis. For nearly as long as the problem has been recognised, climate policies have centred upon the neoliberal orthodoxies of market solutions and individual behaviour change, centring responsibility for tackling climate change upon the people least responsible for causing it while leaving the real culprits unrestrained. This is the intended consequence of vested interests trying to maintain their power and profitability. After decades of big polluters propagating active climate denial and doubt mongering, we now live in the era of deflection and delay. The result is the same: emissions keep soaring.

As the cost-of-living crisis bites and more people experience declining living standards, compulsions to "save energy", "fly less" or "eat less meat" risk ringing hollow – if not actively antagonistically – in the ears of the people who have a growing awareness that the distribution of emissions (which parallels the distribution of wealth) does not point the finger of blame at the average UK citizen. According to Oxfam, it takes a billionaire just 2.78 hours to emit as much as the average British person does in a lifetime.[173] People who are already struggling to make ends meet and have increasingly rubbish lives – in which occasional takeaways and trips to the cinema are entering the realm of unjustifiable luxury – are not likely to warmly welcome what they perceive to be further curbs on comforts and material interest in the face of a 1 per cent able to continue throwing money at wanton overconsumption.

There are tensions here. Firstly, the easiest parts of decarbonisation in the UK have already been achieved – most notably virtually eliminating coal from our energy mix, with an outright majority of our electricity generated from renewable sources some days. But from the perspective of you or me, switching on the light switch in the lounge is exactly the same. The majority of remaining emissions cuts, however, will be noticed one way or the other: how we get around, what we eat, how we heat our homes and so on. Articulating a plan for this decarbonisation in a way which is not just acceptable but desirable to a majority of ordinary people will be a key task of Polanski's Greens.

At the same time, political opponents lined up behind the interests of the 1 per cent are ready to mobilise their base over the first suggestion of state intervention or the mere principle of restrictions on consumption or behaviour. But state-enforced redistribution will necessarily play a growing role in an ecosocialist future – or indeed any future in which states are forced to manage the escalating climate crisis in some manner. Consider the oil crisis of 2026 provoked by the Iran War. In the context of an absolute shortage of something like jet fuel, we are presented with two options: either leave the market to it, allowing the rich to keep jetting around while literally millions of ordinary holidaymakers have their flights cancelled, or have the state intervene to distribute resources in such a way to provide a minimum level of access to travel for as many people as possible. Which of these is the more preferable?

Happily, an analysis of the inequality at play in both wealth and resource use permits Greens to tell an attractive story of democratic redistribution. Globally speaking, Oxfam has also calculated that the richest 1 per cent are responsible for the same amount of emissions as a full two-thirds of the rest of humankind. Not only that, but "a 60 percent tax on the incomes of the richest 1 percent would cut emissions by more than the total emissions of the UK and raise $6.4 trillion a year".[174] Put simply: if the super rich were constrained, there would be more to go around for everyone else, whether that's in terms of direct investment of wealth in the public realm or real planetary resources. This is why the political representatives of the super rich cling tenaciously to the status quo. Contrary to the belief that climate action will make ordinary people's lives worse, standards of living and quality of life will likely improve for the great numbers of us.

An example of this can be seen in the need to cut aviation emissions, which are presently nowhere near on track to meet our climate targets. There are no technological solutions on the horizon and fewer flights must be taken in the immediate term. However, the resulting commonsense and commonplace imperative to "stop flying" because it is "bad" completely flattens and ignores the extremely inequitable distribution of flights (and hence emissions) where 70 per cent of flights are taken by just 15 per cent of us, and half of us don't fly at all in any given year.[175] Private jets are particularly egregious: up to 30 times more polluting than an ordinary flight but usually taxed at a lower marginal rate.[176] A fairer distribution of aviation emissions would mean that some people – such as those who have been starved of a week's summer holiday for years on end – may well end up flying *more*.

Greens have always argued that the problems of climate change and nature degradation require a systemic, political solution, rather than an aggregation of individual efforts to reduce personal emissions and impacts. Jean Lambert remembers Jonathon Porritt saying decades ago that there is little value in a campaign to save the mackerel one year, save the carp the next year, and then save the salmon the year after that, going on endlessly. Instead, what is needed is a political economy which stops putting the natural world under such stress. This was the precise reason for setting up Green parties in the first place.

The timing of the founding of Green parties around the world – in the late 1960s and early 1970s – was a fortuitously contingent moment in many respects. Environmental concern in advanced capitalist economies was high, following major cultural interventions like Rachel Carson's *Silent Spring*, published in 1962 (provoking a successful campaign leading to the phase-out of certain harmful pesticides), and, six years later, in 1968, the first full photographs of Earth from space, stimulating a new planetary consciousness. In 1970 came the first ever Earth Day, inspiring some 20 million US citizens to take to the streets in opposition to environmental destruction. Through the decade came the explosion of NGOs, including Greenpeace and Friends of the Earth here in the UK in the early 1970s. Along with this, often acting as a catchment for the tributaries of related social movements, came the formation of Green parties.

Above all else, what defined this period of environmental activism was Western governments' ideological willingness to take regulatory action, constraining corporate activity to a degree that produced real effects: the termination of acid rain, the banning of harmful chemicals, and the cleaning of our air and oceans. Most notable of this was the founding of the US Environmental Protection Agency, making these sorts of interventions in the heart of American capitalism. The high point and last hurrah of this era of environmental protection came in the form of action taken to repair the ozone layer, the result of a global agreement to ban CFCs (chlorofluorocarbons, the offending synthetic chemical compound) signed in Montreal in 1987. By March 2025, it was confirmed that the ozone was actively healing as a direct consequence of these bans and is projected to be back at 1980 levels by 2040.[177]

This wave of environmental concern and responsive government action was to crash headlong into an ideological revolution which has endured until this day. From the 1980s onwards came the hegemony of neoliberal politics, casting aside the social democratic settlement which had been in place since the Second World War. Rather than interventionist states with ambitious public investment came governments which wanted to shrink public spending, cut red tape and let markets rip. Critically to this story, any sort of regulation placed upon business was considered to be an anathematic market distortion. This marked the end of the willingness to bluntly ban, limit or regulate environmental harms. The conjunction of this rightwing political hegemony with the emergent scientific understanding of climate change is what Naomi Klein has called "an epic case of bad timing".[178] Instead of straightforward state intervention on the climate crisis, we entered the era of market solutions and individual behaviour change.

The author Adrienne Buller has produced one of the most comprehensive critiques of market solutions to the climate crisis in her book *The Value of a Whale* – its title taken from the attempt made by the International Monetary Fund to place a monetary value on a whale, balancing its capacity to generate tourism and sequester carbon with the cost of conservation ($2m per specimen, if you're wondering).[179] This stands as the grotesque logical end point of an approach to tackling the climate crisis based on cap-and-trade schemes, offsetting and carbon prices. Basically, that is to say, to do anything except changing any of the fundamentals of the prevailing economic model which got us into this mess. "There is no way to create markets for nature that can slow the precipitous decline we're facing," Buller tells me. "These are not 'investable' assets in anything like the traditional sense demanded by the thirst for high returns." The results of this ideological approach are now manifest. A 25-year study of carbon offsets, for example, has demonstrated that the schemes have failed to slow heating owing to "intractable" systemic problems.[180]

The 2008 financial crisis opened space for a potential escape from this world of dead end "green capitalist" solutions. Caroline Lucas was among a number of politicians and economists who had drawn up a proposal known as the "Green New Deal", echoing the New Deal which President Roosevelt put into place as a response to the Great Depression of the 1930s. Harking back to the social democratic consensus of the post-war period, the Green New Deal called for Keynesian investment to stimulate the economy through the creation of green jobs across renewables, home insulation and so on. This call became the primary organising principle of the climate movement for the entire 2010s. In 2026, it can be argued that the prevalent economic conditions (chiefly the absence of the late 2010s' near negative interest rates, making government borrowing to invest historically attractive) has at least somewhat compromised this relatively moderate, social democratic conception of a Green New Deal. Time is also wearing on. Today we need to rediscover some of the characteristics states were happier to exhibit back when Green parties were first founded: muscular intervention, no-nonsense regulation and ambitious redistribution. In another case of epic bad timing, however, we must do so in a world where a Trump White House is laying waste to the environmental regulatory framework like never before: repealing the landmark ruling that greenhouse gases are harmful to public health and delaying the phase-out of "super pollutants".[181]

From the 1970s to the present day, Greens are to be credited for their prescient claim that our prevalent economic model is incompatible with planetary conditions which sustain life. Techno-optimists believe that a magic silver bullet solution (carbon capture, green jet fuel, nuclear fusion) will deliver us from disaster, claiming for such technology a tantalising imminence which has persisted, in the face of all available evidence, for many decades. Still we wait. Technocrats believe that tweaking incentives in a largely unreformed economy will be enough to limit waste and pollution. Both are wrong and will lead us boldly into the future of a hothouse earth. The Greens have grasped a truth that the rest of the political establishment will not accept: that an economy built on a cycle of perpetual extraction, production and waste in pursuit of endless economic growth simply cannot obtain forever. Contrary to the vain hopes of market dogmatists, the environmental crisis is at root an economic problem.

An emergent tradition of alternative economics has thus surrounded the Greens. In the earliest years of the party, the impulse towards decentralisation was at its purest and most primitivist, with publications like the foundational *Blueprint for Survival* advocating a belief that humans can only flourish in extremely small, local and self-sustaining communities which are effectively a self-contained economic unit. In 1973, the economist E. F. Schumacher published his essay collection *Small Is Beautiful* based on his expertise in village-based economies, decrying the "giantism" prevalent in an economy tending towards globalisation.[182] While to an extent endorsing the economic position of deep ecologists in the early Green Party in its advocacy for smallness and localism, it nonetheless advanced other core arguments which would resonate even more strongly within Green thought through the decades ahead: most crucially a robust critique of an economy which was geared up to pursue profit above people's well-being.

For all of its subsequent existence as a national political party, the Green Party has accepted that grappling with the workings of a national and global economy is both necessary and desirable. In the mid- to late 1970s, this took the form of advocacy for a "steady state" economy, as described by economist Herman Daly in a series of books published throughout that decade. The central insight of Daly's work was to situate the human economy within the living world, observing that the economy is sustained by the raw materials provided by nature, and that economic activity in turn creates waste and pollution which must be absorbed by the natural world. Given that the planet has a finite number of natural resources and a finite carrying capacity for waste and pollution, this economic model cannot continue indefinitely. What is needed is an economy which balances economic activity with the planet's ability to withstand it. Daly's resulting political views, however, were more in keeping with the Malthusian instincts of the deep ecologists (he advocated, for example, for issuing a fixed number of reproduction licences to fertile women, in order to stabilise the population).

Notwithstanding these political views, Daly's work gave rise to decades of further development of ecological economics, of which one of the most well-known strands is the degrowth movement, which holds that – further to displacing the imperative for endless economic growth – ecological principles demand that some advanced economies must actively shrink. This view is not encoded in Green Party policy, which instead takes the position of being "agnostic" about growth. What is meant by this is that Greens recognise that some activities which are desirable (such as the manufacturing and roll-out of renewable energy infrastructure) would likely stimulate conventional economic growth. A dogmatic application of degrowth – in which the primary economic goal would be to shrink the economy – would therefore technically take a dim view of such a policy. Instead, Greens argue that government decisions should largely disregard the effects they would have on growth either way, in favour of other measures of economic success such as the positive impact on planetary health and the well-being of people. Some of the contributions adjacent to the degrowth movement, therefore, have resonated strongly with Greens. *Post-Growth Living* by Kate Soper, for example, outlines a vision for a society in which material consumption is no longer the dominant basis of our pleasure and argues for a world with more free time, closer communities and so on.[183] Such a vision is manifested through a spectrum of flagship Green policies across its history, from the decentralised localism of its origins, to the four-day week and the 15-minute city of today.

That key imperative to "be agnostic about growth" appears as a chapter title in the book *Donut Economics* by Kate Raworth, which can be considered the most distinguished yet accessible twenty-first-century upgrade on the "steady state" economics for which the Greens had been advocating since the 1970s. The titular doughnut is a visual metaphor for the economy Raworth envisions: a hole in the middle into which nobody should fall (e.g., the floor of meeting everyone's needs) but neither going beyond the outer boundary of the doughnut, past planetary limits. Instead, our economy should reside within the "sweet spot" of the doughnut itself.[184]

How to get to that sweet spot? In recent decades, the minimum economic programme for the Greens has been to deliver a break from the market dogma of Thatcherism and neoliberalism and has been broadly supportive of a return to something like the post-war social democratic consensus of high tax and high spending from an interventionist state. This was most obviously on display in the 2010s in the party's anti-austerity position, combined with the state investment programme advocated through the Green New Deal. In seeking this, Greens recognise that our current economic settlement – to use the doughnut metaphor – is subjecting a growing number of people to the fate of falling into the hole of deprivation, while simultaneously blasting way past planetary limits. This needs urgent correction. But to stay within the doughnut for good? That would require an economy subject to planning and democratic control. That is to say: ecosocialism.

"We live in rip-off Britain," began a speech given by Polanski in March 2026. "Sky high bills, stagnating wages, extreme inequality – it can't go on like this." This was the keynote address at an event celebrating the fortieth anniversary of the New Economics Foundation (NEF), in which Polanski set out some of the principles of what inevitably got termed "Zackonomics". It attempted to tackle a key strategic question: what should the Green economic offer look like in this particular political moment?

Drawing upon the input of economists like Joseph Stiglitz and Mariana Mazzucato, Polanski again charted the contours of eco-populism: noting, for example, that while oil companies scoop up a windfall from war, normal people are subjected to energy price spikes in cold, draughty homes. This should be remedied by direct transfers of wealth from the profiteers and polluters to the wider population. Fossil fuel racketeering like this was given as just one example of clear injustice within a speech which more broadly told the 40-year story of how Thatcherism sold off our public assets, only for a rentier class to sell them back to us at extortionate rates. Polanski promised a break from this consensus with an economic plan built upon three pillars: tackling the cost-of-living crisis, overhauling the tax system to make the super rich pay their fair share, and modernising fiscal policy to meet the challenges of today. Specific proposals included the vaunted wealth tax, equalising capital gains with income tax and junking fixed fiscal rules in favour of a board of "fiscal referees": experts who would be tasked with ensuring the government was spending neither too much, *nor too little* – and took into account multiplier effects for investment which extend beyond a five-year window, as is currently practice.

What the speech demonstrated perhaps above all else was Polanski's understanding of the political need for a laser-like focus on the affordability crisis. "I recognise talking about the future won't reassure people who want to know if they can afford their bills tomorrow," he told his audience. "Struggling families are seeing price rises coming towards them like a freight train, hurtling down the tracks, while they're stuck, helpless and unable to see a way out. Meanwhile, some are profiting from this misery." In this, he shares a key similarity with the mayor of New York, Zohran Mamdani, with whom he is often compared, primarily for their politics, presentation and communications style. In this lesser discussed regard, they also share the insight that their wider political objectives can only be achieved on condition of successfully convincing the electorate that there is a credible plan to alleviate the affordability crisis which is dominating their lives. In Polanski's speech, this meant windfall taxes, rent controls and price caps. What he promised in return were things he remembered as being normal in his childhood: the ability to go on family summer holidays, a rainy-day fund, a coffee on the way to work.

"What I wanted to do in that speech," Polanski reflects,

> is tell this story about rip-off Britain, the story of people being squeezed, of corporations destroying our environment. And I wanted to set out what our economic vision of the country looks like when we're taxing wealth, when we're nationalising our utilities, when we're rolling back neoliberalism, and creating a positive alternative. People living a beautiful, good life where they're able to enjoy the time that they have with friends, family, loved ones. Where we're not constantly in a position of fear, or fighting the climate crisis. Where we're not just trying to survive – we're thriving.

Polanski is correct to focus on affordability. It has never made less sense to talk about the cost of living, on one hand, and the environment, on the other. The issues are now completely entwined. Not least because the ascendant reactionary right presents climate action as being in outright contradiction with ordinary people's economic interests. As Matthew T. Huber writes, in *Climate Change as Class War*, "Class politics is already central to the climate struggle … if you are on the right. In resisting policy, those resistant to climate action consistently cite the economic costs of climate policy – specifically how climate action would lead to job loss, higher energy bills, and pain for working people."[185] This argument takes on more explosive power in the post-Covid context of there being about 10 per cent of the population now actively drawn to social media-fuelled conspiratorial thinking.[186] And as the director of Persuasion UK, Steve Akehurst, put it to me: "The radical right has eaten the centre-right in most advanced economies in the world. Anti-net zero positioning is one of the things that has been weaponised in that regard." When these forces provoke mobilisation, the results are ugly.

In February 2023, thousands of protesters gathered in the typically demure city of Oxford, among them elements of the far-right group Patriotic Alternative, with reports of some chanting "Jews will not replace us" and "refugees are rapists". What they were protesting, astonishingly, was the introduction of half a dozen bus gates.[187] This far-right backlash later took a step into the political mainstream when Labour lost a by-election in the outer London constituency of Uxbridge during the height of the furore about Mayor Sadiq Khan's expansion of the Ultra Low Emissions Zone (a proposed surcharge on the dirtiest cars driven within a given zone). The dominant (if oversimplistic) interpretation was that environmental policy was electoral poison. It was then open season on anything net zero: sitting government ministers peddled conspiracy theories; the then prime minister Rishi Sunak gave a set piece speech trashing climate policy; and the succeeding Conservative leader Kemi Badenoch pledged to repeal the Climate Change Act.[188]

"There is an electoral logic to all this specifically within the right of British politics," Akehurst tells me. "If you look at voters on the right, particularly voters that went to Reform, the intensity of opposition to net zero has increased slightly. It still only amounts to 25 per cent of the public, but it's a majority of people who have gone from the Conservatives to Reform." This fight for a core vote on the right of electoral politics is having an outsized impact on public discourse, inflated by an establishment media pushing an anti-net zero bias which is demonstrably out of alignment with majority public opinion.[189] Most notably, this process has spooked the Labour Party, despite the fact that very few Labour voters are switching directly to Reform, and certainly not owing to Farage's ministrations about scrapping net zero. Polanski offers a politics that pushes back on this doom loop, promoting climate solutions which can bring down the cost of living. This has the potential to build broad coalitions within the majority of the public still openly supportive of climate action, while potentially peeling away the significant proportion of Reform voters who prioritise economic justice far more highly than ideological opposition to net zero.

Take energy as an example of the terrain upon which a distorted public and political discourse can be reoriented towards popular support for climate action. The gas crisis of 2022 provoked by the Russian invasion of Ukraine exposed the vulnerabilities to which UK consumers are subject when we are so reliant on fossil fuels. Contrary to the claims of climate deniers and delayers, high energy costs in the UK are not a consequence of green levies but are in fact primarily because the price of electricity in the UK is pegged to the price of gas, which is used as the energy of last resort. That means that if even 1 per cent of our electricity is generated by gas, it sets the price of 100 per cent of it. And that means that if the price of gas goes through the roof, energy bills follow. Owing to the illegal Iran War, we stand on the precipice of a fossil fuel crisis which threatens to recast 2022 as a mere ripple. The Climate Change Committee has warned that the cost of a single further energy price shock is likely to be greater than the entire price tag for hitting net zero.[190]

One part of the solution to this is clean, cheap energy. As is now widely demonstrated, the cost of generating electricity from renewables is significantly lower than generating electricity from fossil fuels. Thrown to the mercy of unrestrained market forces, however, we are unlikely to see the requisite improvement in people's material conditions alongside the deep emissions cuts we need to achieve. This is argued in Brett Christophers' *The Price Is Wrong*, in which he explains that owing to their lack of scarcity and inability to be commodified, renewables are simply not profitable enough to stimulate the necessary private capital investment.[191] Only states can pump in the requisite funding to roll out the clean energy needed while actively shutting down fossil fuel production. That means the second component of getting out of this trap of high energy costs is a democratically owned energy sector which is no longer subordinated to the profit motive. Something very much like this is already popular. Over two-thirds of people support a nationalised energy sector relative to around 18 per cent of people who oppose it.[192] This was exactly the sort of thing Polanski was proposing in his speech.

In addition to all this, climate breakdown is now actively *driving* the cost-of-living crisis, as has been argued by James Meadway, economist and co-director of Green Party adjacent think tank Verdant.[193] Drought, extreme heat and extreme rainfall around the world are wrecking harvests, decimating livestock and sending food prices through the roof. Even if we stopped emitting carbon overnight, this will only get worse in the medium term, and history is littered with governments toppled by the price of rice and bread. The price of eggs was a key political factor in the defeat of Biden and the re-election of Trump. Even the *Telegraph* has conceded that our own government could be brought down by stubborn food inflation, invoking images of food riots through the centuries.[194] A mooted solution was to further liberalise world trade to allow more cheap imports. But in the context of the rising possibility of shocks visited upon the entire globalised system of trade – from the fact that 60 per cent of food is produced in just five countries, to the far-reaching effects of key shipping routes being closed – the article of faith that free markets can always produce cheap goods is fast colliding with ecological reality.[195]

As we were constantly reminded throughout Covid: once presented with a crisis, things that we had endlessly been told were impossible can suddenly become inevitable. In May 2026, the *Financial Times* reported that the Treasury was pushing UK supermarkets to cap the prices of some such essentials (in return, it was reported, for cutting or delaying other regulations).[196] Supermarket fat cats, and their free-market outriders, dutifully flooded the media to decry the idea as "crazy", and it took just one day for Reeves to buckle and rule it out.[197] This is, however, the sort of policy which will be necessary to protect citizens from the series of shocks which await us in the months, years and decades ahead. That is to say: the political courage to constrain profiteering. In the same week, across the Atlantic, Mayor Mamdani announced his plans to open a series of state-owned grocery stores with lower prices. The first was to be opened in the low-income neighbourhood of the Bronx.[198]

Back during the Green Party leadership election, on the *Jeremy Vine* show, Reem Ibrahim, from the rightwing libertarian think tank the Institute of Economic Affairs, scoffed at Polanski suggesting that food is a human right, and sneeringly asked if he was going to nationalise Sainsbury's.[199] She had in fact put her finger on a very good idea. As Meadway has noted, Morrisons is set to close over 100 stores.[200] These could be purchased by the government to kick start a fledgling chain of state-run supermarkets.[201] Imagine coupling this with a plan to revitalise the network of publicly owned "council farms" which were established in the late nineteenth century but have been halved since the 1970s owing to the pernicious effects of privatisation and cuts.[202] Restoring and expanding such a network could support nature, create jobs and contribute to the supply chains of non-profit state-run supermarkets. The delivery of such a suite of policies to create a more self-sufficient Britain which provided affordable access to decent food for its population would be to realise ambitions of some of the earliest Green Party manifestos. It would also meet head on today's affordability crisis.

If the environment seems obscured within the Green Party's priorities today, it's because it has rightly been absorbed within their broader political and economic offer. From long before his leadership campaign, one of Polanski's most oft-repeated phrases was that "there is no environmental justice without social, economic and racial justice too". This phrase is not just an assertion of the party's long-held values. It's now as much a pragmatic and politically strategic claim. It is obviously the case that we cannot endure an economy which benefits a small elite of people at the expense of the planet, undermining the life source of everything upon which we depend. Equally though, nor can we create environmental policy which immiserates people and expect populations to maintain their support for such policies endlessly. The only route forward is a politics which privileges both people and planet, correctly seeing humans as part of the nature within which we are situated.

Undoubtedly, Polanski has foregrounded a traditional economic class antagonism to his presentation of the Greens' programme, as is correct on its own terms, and makes strategic political sense in a period of extreme inequality and intensifying economic stress for growing numbers of people. This inequality is both a symptom and cause of environmental degradation, with the 1 per cent disproportionately responsible for the emissions and resource use which is condemning our planet and everything on it. The Wealth Gap Risk Register produced by the Fairness Foundation has found that "increased wealth inequality is directly correlated with higher per capita carbon dioxide emissions".[203] It is both politically necessary and politically expedient to tackle this problem.

Reconstituting the 99 per cent around a politics which permits a liveable future will require a majority of the popular classes to believe that green policy can improve their material conditions: cutting the price of food, transport, heating and energy. This can only be achieved by displacing the primacy of the profit motive within our economy. Reform and the far right win when people and the planet are siloed, allowing them to be presented as mutually exclusive priorities in a zero-sum game. In their telling, the working class loses out in favour of global elites hiking taxes on ordinary people while the planet goes on burning. In fact, the opposite is true. It's climate change that will make things more expensive, not the action to tackle it. And while constraining the profligate consumption of the super rich is a prerequisite of tackling climate change, it can also help fund an economic transition that benefits the majority of the population. In the end, the climate crisis and the cost-of-living crisis are indivisible symptoms of failing capitalism. The solutions also overlap. When Polanski talks about a wealth tax, he's talking about the environment.

CONCLUSION

The Battle for Britain's Future

The greatest test of Polanski's leadership to date came with the elections of May 2026. The test was twofold. Most obviously it was his first major electoral challenge: a national election in Wales, and over 5,000 council seats contested across England (a national election in Scotland, which concerned the separate Scottish Greens, was also held on the same day). In addition, the campaign also represented the most violent assault yet on an ascendent Green Party by political opponents, with attacks reaching a degree of intensity more commonly associated with the leader of an opposition party in a general election.

For the first six months or so of Polanski's leadership, attacks from the billionaire press had been recast as a virtue and skilfully turned to Polanski's advantage: presented to supporters as evidence that the political challenge to vested interests was real, and used as recruitment and propaganda material across social media. The *Daily Mail* splash of "the Green menace" was memed and parodied to death by supporters.[204] But in the week or so before the May elections, Polanski and the Greens got a taste of what it was like when the smear machine really turned the heat up. It wasn't pretty.

It is important to concede that a small number of Green candidates who were standing in the local elections made unmistakably antisemitic remarks. But to say that the resulting campaign from Labour and the rightwing media was a disproportionate overreach would be an understatement. A dossier of attacks against individual candidates utilised by London Labour the day before the election included the handful of these antisemitic candidates. It also included, for example, someone who they alleged had been arrested for direct action with Just Stop Oil (a claim deleted after legal action was threatened) and people who had supported Bob Vylan's "death to the IDF [Israel Defense Forces]" chant. Most shocking of all was a social media post aimed at a candidate named Carlotta Allum, who was used as a drugs mule several decades ago, collaborated in putting the offending drug dealer behind bars, and now runs a charity supporting people in similar situations.[205] Labour reduced this woman's experience to having "served a prison sentence in the US for smuggling 10,000 ecstasy tablets" on a social media graphic of a vulgar, mocked-up pastiche of a detective's case file.

The legacy media dutifully played its part. Deputy leader Rachel Millward was hauled over the coals for tweeting that a third victim of the perpetrator of the horrific Golders Green attacks – a Muslim – was rarely mentioned in the resultant coverage and commentary. This was alleged to be "conspiracy theory" in a full-length article by the *Telegraph*, an allegation which stretched the commonly understood meaning of "conspiracy theory" to breaking point given that Millward's claim carried the virtue of being verifiably true.[206]

All of this played out in a climate of heightened tension and moral confusion, with some unprecedented interventions from the establishment which had the effect (in some cases undoubtedly deliberately) of blurring the lines between fair criticism of Israel, Palestinian solidarity and clear cases of antisemitism. The commissioner of the Metropolitan Police took to the broadcast media to condemn Palestinian march organisers for seeking to march past synagogues. What was meant by this, as it turned out, was that the planned assembly point for marches – a routinely chosen spot for mass assemblies in the heart of central London, outside BBC Broadcasting House – was a couple of streets away from a synagogue.[207] The Conservative leader of the opposition, Kemi Badenoch, spent a media cycle calling for a ban on pro-Palestine marches but made a specific point of saying that such a ban ought not to be applied to far-right marches organised by Tommy Robinson on the basis that they did not create a climate of fear and intimidation aimed at anyone in particular.[208] Some people may justifiably feel otherwise. At the Unite the Kingdom rally of September 2025, a MAGA activist, Valentina Gomez, spoke from the main stage lamenting that "they took your guns, they took your swords, and they raped your women" and called upon the assembled tens of thousands to "fight for this nation or let all of these rapist Muslims and corrupt politicians take over".[209]

Polanski's response to the focussed attacks on the Greens, and the wider political atmosphere, can be judged in one regard as some improvement on the similar situation in which Jeremy

Corbyn found himself towards the end of the 2010s: the Greens swiftly suspended the candidates for the egregious examples of clear antisemitism while Polanski publicly condemned them and implored the public not to vote for them. At the same time, he took a more robust and sophisticated line on defending the party more widely and made very clear that there should be no conflation between criticism of Israel and antisemitic targeting of Jews. In doing so, he exposed the media's ingrained hostility on this question. Polanski put it to Trevor Phillips on Sky News that the legitimacy of his own Jewish perspective was being dismissed in this conversation. "Don't try that one on me," came Phillips' unspeakably patronising response.[210] For all this, Polanski effectively achieved the opposite of what Labour managed under Corbyn, which was to drag their heels on taking action against offending members while sending mixed messages on the national stage.

On the other hand, it would be fair to say that Polanski made some missteps which fanned the flames that licked around him. Most notably, the choice to retweet criticism of police violence inflicted against the Golders Green stabber was, whatever you think of the legitimacy of the point being made, undoubtedly an unforced error in terms of raw political calculation. It dominated the media cycle thereafter, in a week when the clear strategic imperative was to move the conversation away from the allegation of antisemitism within the Greens and back onto the core messages of the cost of living. On the *Today* programme the morning before polling day, Polanski was trapped by one of his primary strengths: his willingness to calmly give a straight answer to anything asked of him. Rather than riding the momentum provided by their astonishing projected results, Polanski was answering questions about his own past and allegations of antisemitism.[211] It did not help matters that he also misspoke live on air, claiming that the assailant was handcuffed while he was being kicked by police when he was not. This provoked a fresh wave of media scrutiny in the few precious hours remaining before polls opened. On *Peston* on ITV that night, Polanski was engaged in a somewhat academic conversation about whether Israel – or indeed any country – has the right to exist.[212] As the country woke to cast their vote, segments of the online Left were pontificating about the distinction between sovereignty of a nation and sovereignty of a people. This was not exactly a glorious echo of the swelling optimism and hope which characterised the crescendo of Labour's 2017 general election campaign. It was closer to the interminable, inwards-looking culture which had been shrinking the political horizons of Your Party over the preceding six months.

By any fair assessment of the situation, the Greens had somewhat lost the media narrative by election day. Contrast Reform's vile deployment of a policy to situate detention centres in Green constituencies which, whether or not it might have had some self-defeating political dimensions, undoubtedly seized the initiative and set an agenda on their own terms. For the Greens, however, you might weigh the balance between self-inflicted damage and a coordinated smear campaign, the main thing that matters is the result: a 14-point percentage drop in approval ratings for Polanski as reported by More in Common in the week of the elections.[213] Moreover, this drop was not primarily contained within segments of the population obviously hostile to anti-police rhetoric but within soft-left demographics, which were the obvious groups within which to expand beyond the existing Green base.[214] With ambition to build a left project with popular appeal, this is cause for concern. And all of this was but a taste of what awaits Polanski and the Greens should they be enjoying remotely similar polling numbers when the general election approaches.

Reflecting on the spate of sting stories about him, Polanski told me:

> I think it's a bad faith attack when anyone suggests that all these things are just happening to come to the surface, as opposed to there having been a very coordinated smear campaign. Funded and operated by the rightwing media, they find things which, in and of themselves, are completely trivial and meaningless. But they add up to create a tapestry that allows journalists to keep asking someone repeatedly on broadcast if they can be trusted, as if the media isn't part of the machine that's undermining that trust.

What does he intend to do about it? "I think we really need to have a conversation about media reform," Polanski says.

> Journalism is a noble profession, but a tiny number of multimillionaires and billionaires have a monopoly on our media. I think politicians have sometimes been nervous of making that argument because you can sound like a sore loser. But actually, I think the public gets it. They get that the media lies to them all the time. And so I think rather than just criticising the media, we need to be pushing for better solutions. We've

> also got to build around the media, which is why I have my podcast, which is why I've written a book, which is why we make social media content to connect with people directly about what the truth is, arming our own activists with rebuttals to lies or smears.

"My final self-reflection," he concludes, "is to sharpen up even further. You can always be better as a communicator."

On the straight electoral test, Polanski and the Greens passed with flying colours. As we saw in Chapter 6, May 2026 represented the best ever set of local election results the party had ever achieved, making incredible advances across former Labour strongholds in inner cities, while still going forwards in the more small-c conservative, rural areas, which some feared would recoil and fall away under a left populist national programme.

The Greens won 587 seats (a net gain of 441), taking control of five councils and winning two directly elected mayors for the first time.[215] In Wales, they broke onto the Senedd, taking two new Greens to the nation's capital.[216] Their vote share went up almost everywhere; their ability to make even more gains often thwarted by the distortions of first past the post. The BBC, when it converted the English results into a projected national vote share, put the Greens in second place on 18 per cent.[217] In doing this, Greens took (excluding mayoral contests) 1.95 million votes – nearly double their previous record of 2023, and even a fraction higher than the last general election, with its much larger electorate. The Greens also won the popular vote in well over a dozen places: 44 per cent in Norwich, 43 per cent in Hackney, 42 per cent in Hastings. All of this points towards the strong prospects of parliamentary breakthroughs in 2029 in diverse places way beyond your Brightons and Bristols. The results also reinforced the sense in which the new contours of English politics are shaped around a straight battle between Greens and Reform. In Sheffield, for instance, the Greens took 27.5 per cent of the vote while Reform took 26.4 per cent – now a knife-edge battleground. Labour came in third. As these results trickled in over the weekend, Polanski took to the airwaves to proclaim, with some justification, that two-party politics was "dead and buried". He might be right.

That said, the advances of Reform cannot be glossed over, winning an eye-watering 1,454 seats – nearly all net gains. Small consolations could be found in the fact that this arguably fell slightly short of highest expectations and represented a fall in vote share relative to the local elections of 2025. Extrapolated to a national vote, these results would put Reform on course to be the biggest party, rather than win an outright majority – progress of a sort. These Reform gains went to show that, while Chapter 6 argued that Greens can win anywhere *in principle*, they cannot yet win everywhere at scale in practice. A perfect example of this was Wigan, a Labour town which fell entirely to Reform.

There are nonetheless some shoots of optimism to be found here. Firstly, as Ben Walker of the *New Statesman* has argued, there are grounds to believe that the Greens are indeed peeling voters directly from Reform, primarily on the basis of the strong malevolence towards the entire political system shared by both groups of voters.[218] Furthermore, as concluded by research into post-industrial England conducted by Common Wealth, "contrary to common assumptions, the most promising progressive strategy for post-industrial areas is not to shift to the right, but to lean into popular economic radicalism through policy interventions anchored in everyday experiences".[219] Taken in combination, these things point to a potential route for Greens to mount a direct challenge to Reform in such places. The prospect of building the necessary organising infrastructure within this election cycle, however, is a much taller task.

The result in Wigan was also an illustration of the fact that nobody had a worse night than Labour. Even the shrunken rump of the Conservative Party could still point to its core voters: pensioners in the south-east. But in shedding their English cities to the Greens, their post-industrial towns to Reform, Wales to Plaid Cymru and Scotland long gone, it really wasn't entirely clear who was now Labour's social base. This was perhaps the final wreckage of the Starmer project.

In February 2023, Keir Starmer stood at a podium flanked by Union Jacks and defiantly said to a crushed Left within his own party that Labour had changed permanently. "If you don't like the changes we've made," he said, "the door is open and you can leave."[220] Many tens of thousands did. One result was possibly the most extraordinary 12 months in the history of the Green Party of England and Wales, and the most abysmal for Labour. Following their worst-ever local election results in 2026, it was down to a rightwing ally of the Starmer project, Luke Akehurst, anticipating a leadership challenge, to tweet into the void: "If you aren't already a member of the Labour Party, you should join now."[221] Some took great pleasure in pointing out to him that, three years prior, they had been told to fuck off. Other Labour figures indulged themselves in vindictive special pleading about how Greens had split the vote on the Left, allowing Reform (who had hoovered up the Conservative vote) to flip countless Labour seats. Such appeals might have met a less hostile reception had they spent any of the preceding years doing anything to court the Greens, rather than sneering at their voters, smearing their candidates and gleefully setting themselves in open opposition to the concerns of environmentalists.

As this book goes to print, Starmer has resigned as leader of the Labour Party, with Andy Burnham his near-certain successor. Famously, Burnham won a decisive by-election victory in Wigan mere weeks after Reform swept the council in the local elections. Some point to this as evidence of Burnham's ability to revive Labour's prospects in such places. Perhaps he can. But it must be conceded that the conditions of the by-election were extraordinary: framed as a referendum on Starmer's premiership, it does not stand as a good proxy for a broader general election performance in which Burnham is a prime minister rather than a local candidate and an insurgent challenger. Time will tell how such a leadership survives contact with state orthodoxies and the Labour machine. Triangulation began before he'd even won the by-election.

All the same, it is in principle possible that, by the 2029 election, or even by the time you read this book, Labour has alighted on some combination of leader, policy programme and communications strategy which has started to reverse their dire polling, and that peak-Polanski might be in the rear-view mirror. It could even be the case that Polanski's leadership is not able to withstand the relentlessness of stories seeking to frame him as untrustworthy or dishonest – especially when this tips into the biggest political sin of all: a perception of hypocrisy. This risks putting a hard ceiling on Polanski's appeal at around a quarter of the most leftwing segment of the electorate, inhibiting his ability to build a working social majority for change with the Greens alone. This points to the strategic need to keep building leading figures around Polanski, such as the brilliant media performer Rachel Millward, the compelling and authentic Mothin Ali, and the rising star of Hannah Spencer to entrench, protect and extend the gains made over the last year. But Polanski's inheritance is as important as his legacy. This book has only in part been about the person currently in the leadership role. Its true subject has been the Green Party of England and Wales, the unique and necessary role it has played in British politics over the last 50 years, and the potential it holds to transform our country in the years ahead. The most important facet of this potential is not Zack Polanski – it's the party's democratic structures, its committed membership, and their undying belief that we can build a fairer society on a safer planet. This will endure beyond any individual leader.

In any event, more likely than a rapid Labour revival is that the multi-party fragmentation of the present moment will persist to some degree through this entire electoral cycle. The local elections resulted in a record number of councils under "no overall control" – a good phrase for the general experience of living in the UK in 2026. Consider the result in Birmingham: Labour losing their dominant majority by shedding 48 seats in every direction.[222] The result was a six-way spread of party representation with just an 11-seat difference between the largest and smallest parties out of a total of 101. Reform, Greens, Labour, Conservative, Independents and Liberal Democrats, all with between 12 and 23 seats, and goodness knows what sort of future governance for a city in crisis. Rather than any reconsolidation of two-party politics, Birmingham City Council feels like the likelier picture of our politics going forward. It is hard to imagine how all of this can continue to endure under conditions of first past the post. The prospect of a sitting government feeling forced to enact proportional representation has never felt so tangible.

But there is little point in further speculating where we might end up by 2029. In the mere six months I spent writing this book in the first half of 2026, Peter Mandelson was revealed to be sharing sensitive state information with a known sex trafficker and paedophile, a former prince was hauled down the cop shop on his birthday, and a war was unleashed in Iran which choked the global oil supply and provoked a fresh, enduring cost-of-living crisis. I was under no particular illusion that our political class was incapable of visiting upon itself a deeper crisis of legitimacy than the one I described in the Introduction, but I must admit that I was nonetheless surprised by a great deal of what unfolded in such a short space of time.

Whatever world you are living in when you are reading this book, and however the Greens are faring in the polls, one thing will remain true: the first year of Polanski's leadership unquestionably delivered a significant impact and lasting legacy. "People ask me what my biggest success has been as leader in the first nine months," Polanski tells me,

> and there's lots to pick from: whether it's record polling, the fifth MP, the two elected mayors, our most successful local elections result ever, or nearly 200,000 new members. But I think one of the biggest successes is the fact that, from Wes Streeting calling for capital gains tax in line with income tax, to Andy Burnham knowing that he needed to talk about reversing neoliberalism, to having a Labour Party kind of flirting with Green Party ideas, we've been significant enough that we've shifted government policy.

If Greens fall back in the polls, this can only be because Polanski has made a leading contribution in wrecking the most unpopular and rightwing Labour government of all time, and forced Starmer's successor to move left rather than punch left. It is, of course, not impossible to imagine that, in the years ahead, the Greens play an active role in extracting a concession from the government which results in the permanent constitutional change of proportional representation. This would be historic. It is also perfectly plausible to picture Polanski leading dozens of new Green MPs into Parliament, holding the balance of power, or even playing a formal role in a rainbow coalition. But perhaps above all else, what Polanski has provided from the moment he stood for leadership of the Green Party in spring 2025 was something for which the Left and the country at large was desperate: a renewed belief that collective, transformational political change was still possible.

If there is one idea or motif which has been central to Polanski's leadership of the Green Party, it can be captured in one word: hope. In this, like so much else, he is in continuity with the recent and deeper past of the Greens, from Petra Kelly taking her place in the German parliament clutching a bouquet of sunflowers to Caroline Lucas addressing her constituents as a newly elected MP, thanking them for choosing the politics of hope over the politics of fear.

There are two ways in which Polanski has evoked the idea of hope. The first is a direct extension of the way in which Lucas herself so frequently used it, which is indebted to the writer Rebecca Solnit, who specifically distinguished hope from optimism. For Solnit, as Lucas so frequently directly quoted, "hope is an axe you break down doors with in an emergency".[223] That is to say, hope is a practice as well as a feeling; the engagement in practical activities which you have grounds to believe will bring about a better world. As opposed to blind optimism where you simply assume, usually from an insulated position of immediate privilege, that everything will somehow turn out all right in the end. Many of us turned to Solnit in the aftermath of the dual shock of Brexit and Trump in 2016. Ten years later, in a world of permanently contested values and a resurgent far right, this appeal to rooting a belief in positive outcomes in practical action is more relevant than ever. This conceptualisation of hope, as earnestly as it is sometimes expressed, provides forceful pushback against the justifiable criticism that "hope" is no substitute for strategy, organisation and hard power. Solnit shows they can overlap.

The second way in which Polanski evokes hope is especially salient in the present moment: the effective opposite of the hopelessness which currently afflicts the country, along with most other late capitalist states of the West. That is to say: hope as the restoration of the mere belief in the principle that things can change for the better, and that politics can be a vehicle for that change. Resurgent waves of left-populism and possibility since the millennium have dashed against the rocks of reality time and time again. Since the Covid disaster of 2020, the energy price and cost-of-living spikes since, and the seemingly near permanent economic emergency installed by the Iran War – the public is now shattered in every sense: exhausted, depleted and fragmented like never before. Polanski is the first leftwing figure in Britain for years who has shown any real sign of having the ability to pull together these fragments of British society into a majoritarian coalition which recognises its shared material interests. Whether this moment is any different to the thwarted promises of the recent past remains to be seen. What we do know, though, is that a mere 12 months ago, entering the 2030s with Nigel Farage in 10 Downing Street seemed to be a near certainty. Many other possible futures now lie before us.

Both of these conceptions of hope have been on full display over the first year of Polanski's leadership, from the activists dancing through the rain on the day they sent a plumber to Parliament, to Polanski himself MC-ing a house set in front of half a million people who came out in the biggest anti-far-right mobilisation in British history. Crucially, these moments combined an effervescent joy with a pipeline into practical political action. It's this which makes Polanski's Greens such a vital political force, giving people concrete ways of building something together, strengthening social movements, winning state power and pushing back on the far right – and all in service of a programme oriented towards ecosocialism. For the Greens this has utopian dimensions, permitting us to catch glimpses of a world of shared abundance, thriving ecology and collective liberation which we could inhabit. But there is also the much more ordinary hope of which Polanski speaks: a life where all of us can enjoy the pleasures of a holiday with our loved ones, seeing the first swallow returning for spring, a rush of feeling on a first date, the collective euphoria of live music and watching your kids do well. A growing number of us can feel that society is straining and know that the planet is in peril. It can be hard to sustain optimism. But for the sake of both utopian dreaming and ordinary hope, we must not succumb to despair. There is far too much to look forward to.

Note on the Text

It is important to make clear my relationship to Zack Polanski, the Green Party of England and Wales and some of the other people discussed in this text.

I have been a member of the Green Party of England and Wales since 2015, and I worked for the party as a member of staff between 2016 and 2021. For the bulk of that time, I worked in the national communications team, but for a period at the end of that term of employment I acted as the communications manager for the 2021 London Mayoral and Assembly elections. Most of my time was taken up by supporting the mayoral candidate Sian Berry (now MP for Brighton Pavilion), but it was during this campaign that I first properly met Zack Polanski, who took a seat on the London Assembly as a consequence of those elections.

I have stayed in touch with Zack (and many other Greens) ever since. In the spring of 2025, I became part of his core campaign team for the party's leadership election on a voluntary basis (as were all the members of the campaign team – no leadership candidates have access to paid staff).

I say this to be upfront about my relationship with Zack and the Greens and to be clear about the position from which I write this book. I have nonetheless done my best to take a robust view of the limitations and challenges facing the Greens, and indeed the broader Left, at this moment of great peril and opportunity. I hope the reader will agree that I have taken the subject matter seriously.

This text has been informed by a number of people who took the time to speak to me during the writing of this book, including Zack himself. Where people are directly quoted without an endnote, such quotations are taken from these original interviews. I thank these people by name in the acknowledgements.

I believe all of the information in this book to be accurate and up to date as of the beginning of June 2026. All referenced links were last accessed in late May 2026. This has been, to say the least, a fast-changing period for the Greens and politics in general – and so some things may have fallen out of date by the time you are reading this, for which I can only apologise.

Aside from some peripheral functionality of everyday software (like Google searches and automatic transcription of voice notes, etc.) no AI has been used in producing the text of this book. Any hallucinations found in these pages are solely the organic hallucinations of a man with three very young children.

Acknowledgements

I am firstly grateful to my loving and supportive parents, Sarah and Trevor.

The greatest thanks of all go to Sam, for everything; the life we share together and for being so wonderful in every way. I love you so much. Thank you also to our three beautiful children for being so inspiring every day, but especially for the nights you went to sleep at a reasonable hour so that I could write this book.

Thank you to the many magnificent teachers at Crickhowell High School who enabled me to write a book 20 years later.

Working with the whole team at Pluto on this project has been a real joy, and I am particularly indebted to David Castle for the belief he showed in me, and this work, and the excellent support he provided throughout the whole process. Thank you also to Rina, Emily, Jonila, Melanie, Jamie and Veruschka.

I am grateful to the many people who took the time to speak to me at length to enrich this text. Thank you to Natalie Bennett,

Michael Chessum, Jean Lambert, Naranee Ruthra-Rajan, Steve Jackson, Paul Valentine, Kate Jones, Alexander Sallons, Chris Williams, Danny Dorling, Jeremy Gilbert, Hau-Yu Tam, Steve Akehurst, Derek Wall and Grace Blakeley. Thank you to the many other sources who provided shorter quotations and background conversations on specific matters.

I am also grateful to the many friends, colleagues and comrades who read early versions of chapters and offered constructive criticism and encouragement. I cannot name all of them – some of them cannot be associated with a writing project of this nature – so I will name none of them. I hope I have shown enough gratitude to you in real life. I am equally grateful, if not more so, to those friends who only pretended to read the drafts I shared but gave me fulsome praise all the same.

Thank you to members of Zack Polanski's team who have been extremely helpful through the writing process, in particular Georgia Nelson and Georgia Elander.

Thank you to Izzy Romilly for taking my photograph so beautifully.

I want to mention the incredible campaign team from the 2025 leadership election, which was one of the best teams and projects I've ever been part of. Shout-out to Naranee, Leda, Steve, Benali, Claudia, Dagan, Erin, Caspar, Paul, Natalia, Callum, Jamie, Joshua and Ruairidh. I am also grateful to the many brilliant colleagues from my time employed by the Green Party and the many amazing politicians and candidates I was fortunate to work with.

I also want to acknowledge the huge wealth of serious thinking and analysis which has sprung up around the Greens over the last year or so, much of it while I was writing this book. Adam Ramsay has long been the closest thing the Greens have to a mainstream pundit and has written much essential reading on the party across various outlets. Two podcasts – Life of the Party and the New Party Podcast – have both engaged in robust and generous discussion about the Greens and the Left, and have been hugely influential on this book. Novara Media and the New Statesman have both covered the Greens seriously and with scrutiny. There is much else out there which has helped inform this text and would make brilliant additional reading for anyone who finds interest in this book.

Of course, a particular thank you is owed to Zack Polanski for sending me a voice note in spring 2025 about a "little project" he was working on, which brought me into his leadership campaign team, and set me on the journey towards the book you are now holding.

Finally, writing this book has renewed my gratitude to the many thousands of people across the country, both within the Green Party and outside it, who work tirelessly in pursuit of a fairer society on a safer planet. This book is offered in hope to all of you.

Notes

1. House of Commons Library. Low growth: The economy's biggest challenge. 16 July 2024. https://commonslibrary.parliament.uk/low-growth-the-economys-biggest-challenge/

2. Stockholm University: Stockholm Resilience Centre (2025) Planetary boundaries. www.stockholmresilience.org/research/planetary-boundaries.html

3. HM Government. Global ecosystem degradation and collapse threaten UK national security and prosperity: A national security assessment. 19 January 2026. www.gov.uk/government/publications/nature-security-assessment-on-global-biodiversity-loss-ecosystem-collapse-and-national-security

4. National Centre for Social Research. Trust and confidence in Britain's system of government at record low. 12 June 2024. https://natcen.ac.uk/news/trust-and-confidence-britains-system-government-record-low

5. National Centre for Social Research. Half of Britain wants

voting system to change, with clear majority among Labour supporters. 22 September 2022. https://natcen.ac.uk/news/half-britain-wants-voting-system-change-clear-majority-among-labour-supporters

6. YouGov. Labour's voter coalition broke more to left than right at 2026 local elections. 21 May 2026. https://yougov.com/en-gb/articles/54811-labours-voter-coalition-broke-more-to-left-than-right-at-2026-local-elections

7. *The New Statesman*. Rishi Sunak boasted of taking money from "deprived urban areas" to help wealthy towns. 5 August 2022. www.newstatesman.com/politics/conservatives/2022/08/exclusive-rishi-sunak-taking-money-deprived-urban-areas

8. Will Snell. The UK's wealth gap has grown by 50% in eight years – and poses a strategic risk to the nation. *LSE Inequalities*. 29 October 2024. https://blogs.lse.ac.uk/inequalities/2024/10/29/the-uks-wealth-gap-has-grown-by-50-in-eight-years/

9. Resolution Foundation. Families have suffered from £20,000 of lost living standards growth over the past 20 years. 18 September 2025. www.resolutionfoundation.org/press-releases/families-have-suffered-from-20000-of-lost-living-standards-growth-over-the-past-20-years/

10. Institute for Fiscal Studies. New statistics show large increases in material deprivation and food insecurity during cost-of-living crisis, which headline poverty measures do not reflect. 21 March 2024. https://ifs.org.uk/news/new-statistics-show-large-increases-material-deprivation-and-food-insecurity-during-cost

11. *The Guardian*. All UK families "to be worse off by 2030" as poor bear the brunt, new data warns. 22 March 2025. www.theguardian.com/uk-news/2025/mar/22/all-uk-families-to-be-worse-

off-by-2030-as-poor-bear-the-brunt-new-data-warns
12. YouGov. How has political opinion changed over 2025? 18 December 2025. https://yougov.com/en-gb/articles/53758-how-has-political-opinion-changed-over-2025
13. More In Common. Shattered Britain. 2025. www.moreincommon.org.uk/research/shattered-britain/
14. *The Times*. The Green Party is soaring in the polls: Who are its supporters? 14 March 2026. www.thetimes.com/comment/columnists/article/green-party-supporters-who-explained-hannah-spencer-3s95jbpbp
15. X. @robfordmancs. 16 May 2025. https://x.com/robfordmancs/status/1923293760684724273
16. Dan Hodges. We should all be in the dock on immigration. *Labour Uncut*. 19 August 2010. https://labour-uncut.co.uk/2010/08/19/we-should-all-be-in-the-dock-on-immigration-says-dan-hodges/
17. OpenDemocracy. Abortion is becoming a new front in Reform UK's culture war. 20 May 2026. www.opendemocracy.net/aabortion-reform-uk-politics-birth-decriminalization-farage/
18. BBC News. Reform pledges to open migrant detention centres in Green-voting areas. 4 May 2026. www.bbc.co.uk/news/articles/c362e9p385yo
19. YouGov. How would Britain vote at the start of 2026? 21 January 2026. https://yougov.co.uk/politics/articles/53923-how-would-britain-vote-at-the-start-of-2026
20. *The Telegraph*. Angry young women are driving men into the arms of cougars. 22 April 2026. www.telegraph.co.uk/news/2026/04/22/angry-young-women-are-driving-men-into-the-arms-of-cougars/

21. YouGov. How would Britain vote at the start of 2026? 21 January 2026. https://yougov.co.uk/politics/articles/53923-how-would-britain-vote-at-the-start-of-2026; *The New Statesman* (2026) Revealed: The new radicalism among young women. 15 April 2026. www.newstatesman.com/politics/polling/2026/04/revealed-the-new-radicalism-among-young-women
22. Keir Milburn, *Generation Left* (Polity, 2019), p. 1
23. *The Guardian*. Young Tories urge party to broaden appeal after rise in voter "crossover" age. 15 August 2024. www.theguardian.com/politics/article/2024/aug/15/young-tories-urge-party-to-broaden-appeal-after-rise-in-voter-crossover-age
24. Phil Burton-Cartledge, "A Conservative Meltdown", in *The Starmer Symptom*, ed. Mark Perryman (Pluto, 2025), p. 118
25. Sky News. Greens overtake Labour in sensational poll. 3 March 2026. https://news.sky.com/story/greens-overtake-labour-in-sensational-poll-13514420
26. Electoral Reform Society. How would each party have done if May's elections were across all of Britain? 18 May 2026. https://electoral-reform.org.uk/how-would-each-party-have-done-if-mays-elections-were-across-all-of-britain/
27. BBC News. Wigan council results. www.bbc.co.uk/news/election/2026/england/councils/E08000010
28. UK Parliament: Notional election for the constituency of Gorton and Denton on 12 December 2019. https://electionresults.parliament.uk/elections/2222
29. BBC News. Sir John Curtice: Greens' win means future of British politics is more uncertain than ever. 27 February 2026. www.bbc.co.uk/news/articles/cwygpdjq9jjo
30. *The Telegraph*. Tim Stanley: British politics has now shifted

irrevocably to the Right. 7 September 2025. www.telegraph.co.uk/news/2025/09/07/british-politics-reform-labour-reshuffle-centre-gone/

31. *The Telegraph*. Polanski falsely claimed to be Red Cross spokesman. 5 May 2026. www.telegraph.co.uk/politics/2026/05/05/polanski-falsely-claimed-to-be-red-cross-spokesman/; *The Telegraph*. Exclusive: Zack Polanski falsely claimed to have worked at the Ministry of Justice. 10 May 2026. www.telegraph.co.uk/politics/2026/05/10/zack-polanski-falsely-claimed-worked-ministry-justice/

32. Labour List. Former NEC member quits party and vows to remove Labour from power. 14 April 2025. https://labourlist.org/2025/04/mish-rahman-resignation-labour-party-nec/

33. Office for National Statistics: Area profile for Gorton and Denton. www.ons.gov.uk/visualisations/customprofiles/build/#E14001251

34. House of Commons Library (2026) Constituency data: Deprivation in England. https://commonslibrary.parliament.uk/research-briefings/cbp-10526/

35. *The Guardian*. "Huge mistake": Labour in turmoil as Burnham blocked from byelection race. 26 January 2026. www.theguardian.com/politics/2026/jan/25/andy-burnham-blocked-from-byelection-race-by-labour-ruling-committee

36. Full Fact. What did Reform UK candidate Matt Goodwin say about Manchester in 2023? 29 January 2026. https://fullfact.org/politics/matt-goodwin-manchester-video/

37. *The Guardian*. Reform and Tories report "family voting" allegations to watchdog. 27 February 2026. www.theguardian.com/politics/2026/feb/27/family-voting-allegations-gorton-and-denton-bye-

lection-tories-reform-watchdog
38. BBC News. No evidence of "family voting" in by-election. 27 March 2026. www.bbc.co.uk/news/articles/clyxeqpzz2no
39. HuffPost. Labour accused of by-election dirty tricks over "fictitious" tactical voting group. 25 February 2026. www.huffingtonpost.co.uk/entry/labour-accused-of-by-election-dirty-tricks-over-fictitious-tactical-voting-group_uk_699f4974e4b0ef1afcc05421
40. *The Guardian*. "We defeated the parties of billionaire donors": Hannah Spencer's victory speech. 27 February 2026. www.theguardian.com/politics/2026/feb/27/hannah-spencer-victory-speech-green-byelection
41. *The Guardian*. "We defeated the parties of billionaire donors": Hannah Spencer's victory speech. 27 February 2026. www.theguardian.com/politics/2026/feb/27/hannah-spencer-victory-speech-green-byelection
42. Opinium. Gorton and Denton constituency poll. 25 February 2026. www.opinium.com/resource-center/gorton-and-denton-constituency-poll/
43. UK Parliament: Somerton and Frome. https://members.parliament.uk/constituency/3735/election/397
44. UK Parliament: Somerton and Frome. https://members.parliament.uk/constituency/3735/election/397
45. *The Telegraph* (2026) Starmer will lose seat if Greens repeat success at general election. 27 February 2026. www.telegraph.co.uk/politics/2026/02/27/starmer-lose-seat-greens-repeat-success-general-election/
46. X @LukeTryl. 27 February 2026. https://x.com/LukeTryl/status/2027244062441378131
47. BBC News. From plumber to Parliament: The Green Party's

new MP. 27 February 2026. www.bbc.co.uk/news/articles/cwygp-3dqenwo

48. Sky News. Greens overtake Labour in sensational poll. 3 March 2026. https://news.sky.com/story/greens-overtake-labour-in-sensational-poll-13514420

49. *The Guardian*. "We can't just talk to the right": What will Labour do now? 3 May 2025. www.theguardian.com/news/ng-interactive/2025/may/03/what-will-labour-do-next-local-elections-reform-uk-left-right

50. BBC News. England local election results 2025. www.bbc.com/news/election/2025/england/results

51. BBC News. Vote 2014. www.bbc.co.uk/news/events/vote2014/england-council-election-results; BBC News. England local election results 2023. www.bbc.co.uk/news/election/2023/england/results

52. BBC News. England local election results 2025. www.bbc.com/news/election/2025/england/results

53. James Schneider, "Building the Party", in *Your Party: The Return of the Left*, ed. Oliver Eagleton (Verso, 2025), p. 43

54. *Rest Is Politics*. We see you Zack Polanski. 2025. www.youtube.com/shorts/2NETON3a5Zs

55. YouGov. Political favourability ratings, July 2025. 16 July 2025. https://yougov.com/en-gb/articles/52586-political-favourability-ratings-july-2025

56. YouGov. Most Britons don't recognise Ed Davey, five years after he was elected Lib Dem leader. 27 August 2025. https://yougov.com/en-gb/articles/52829-most-britons-dont-recognise-ed-davey-five-years-after-he-was-elected-lib-dem-leader

57. JL Partners. Recognition of political figures. 5 May 2026.

www.jlpartners.co.uk/polling-results

58. *The Guardian*. Zack Polanski claims he can "cut through" at Green party leadership hustings focused on how to counter Farage: As it happened. 30 July 2025. www.theguardian.com/politics/live/2025/jul/30/keir-starmer-uk-palestine-statehood-gaza-uk-politics-latest-updates-news

59. *The Guardian*. Zack Polanski pulling away in race to be party leader, senior Greens believe. 17 August 2025. www.theguardian.com/politics/2025/aug/17/zack-polanski-pulling-away-in-race-to-be-party-leader-senior-greens-believe

60. Find Out Now. Green Party leadership election. 1 September 2025. https://findoutnow.co.uk/blog/green-party-leadership-election/

61. Novara Media. Exclusive: Green Party membership surges following Polanski's leadership bid, leaked data suggests. 30 June 2025. https://novaramedia.com/2025/06/30/exclusive-green-party-membership-hits-record-high-since-polanskis-leadership-bid-leaked-data-suggests/

62. Sky News. Zack Polanski elected new Green Party leader: Full announcement and victory speech. 2 September 2025. www.youtube.com/watch?v=_K-CnGgMt-I

63. BBC News. Green Party: Co-leaders hail highest number of councillors. 4 May 2024. www.bbc.co.uk/news/uk-68956733

64. BBC News: Election 2015 www.bbc.co.uk/news/election/2015/results

65. *The Guardian*. Historic win for Greens in tight Brighton race. 7 May 2010. www.theguardian.com/politics/2010/may/07/greens-historic-win-brighton

66. *The Guardian*. Budget 2010: Public sector faces deepest ever

spending cuts. 22 June 2010. www.theguardian.com/uk/2010/jun/22/2010-budget-public-sector-cuts

67. Michael Chessum, *This Is Only the Beginning: The Making of a New Left – From Anti-Austerity to the Fall of Corbyn* (Bloomsbury, 2022)

68. *The Guardian*. Ed Balls risks union anger in push to bolster Labour's economic credibility. 13 January 2012. www.theguardian.com/politics/2012/jan/13/ed-balls-labour-party-economic-redibility

69. BBC Radio 4. Green party leader Natalie Bennett calls for end to austerity. 7 September 2014. www.bbc.co.uk/programmes/p0267plo

70. BBC News. Green Party's Natalie Bennett in anti-migrant violence warning. 17 July 2013. www.bbc.co.uk/news/uk-politics-23343089

71. Green Party of England and Wales. Change the tune. 8 April 2015. www.youtube.com/watch?v=PPgS7p40ERg

72. BBC News. Green party leader stumbles through radio interview. 24 February 2015. www.bbc.co.uk/news/av/uk-politics-31602252

73. *The Guardian*. Green membership surge takes party past Lib Dems and Ukip. 15 January 2015. www.theguardian.com/politics/2015/jan/15/green-party-membership-surge-leaders-debates

74. Channel 4. Labour supporters claim leadership vote "purge". 20 August 2015. www.channel4.com/news/labour-supporters-purged-from-leadership-vote

75. BBC News. Labour leadership results in full. 12 September 2015. www.bbc.co.uk/news/uk-politics-34221155

76. BBC News: Results of the 2017 general election. www.bbc.co.uk/news/election/2017/results

77. Jeremy Gilbert. Labour should have argued against the last 40 years, not just the last ten. *OpenDemocracy*. 15 January 2020. www.opendemocracy.net/en/labour-should-have-argued-against-last-40-years-not-just-last-ten/
78. BBC News. Labour left-wingers angry about being blocked as MP candidates. 16 November 2022. www.bbc.co.uk/news/uk-politics-63636469
79. BBC News: Results of the 2017 general election. www.bbc.co.uk/news/election/2017/results
80. YouGov. Are Britons willing to vote for "Your Party", ahead of its launch conference? 27 November 2025. https://yougov.com/en-gb/articles/53577-are-britons-willing-to-vote-for-your-party-ahead-of-its-launch-conference
81. Find Out Now. Voting intention: Restore Britain and Your Party. 24 February 2026. https://findoutnow.co.uk/blog/voting-intention-restore-britain-and-your-party/
82. UK Green History. Ecology Party Manifesto for a Sustainable Society. 1975. https://green-history.uk/j3/library/doc-archive/file/162-ecology-party-manifesto-for-a-sustainable-society-1975
83. Green Party of England and Wales: Our 2024 General Election Manifesto. 22024. https://greenparty.org.uk/about/our-manifesto/
84. The Ecologist, *A Blueprint for Survival* (Penguin, 1972), p. 15
85. Jonathon Porritt, *Seeing Green: The Politics of Ecology Explained* (Basil Blackwell, 1984), p. 232
86. Porritt, *Seeing Green*, p. 48
87. Porritt, *Seeing Green*, p. 48
88. Chris Saltmarsh, *Burnt: Fighting for Climate Justice* (Pluto, 2021), p. 89

89. Jonathon Porritt. I was arrested at the Palestine Action ban protest – and it all still seems surreal. *The Independent*. 13 August 2025. www.independent.co.uk/voices/palestine-action-ban-protests-parliament-square-arrest-b2806024.html

90. UK Green History. Ecology Party Election Manifesto. 1975. https://green-history.uk/j3/library/doc-archive/file/162-ecology-party-manifesto-for-a-sustainable-society-1975

91. James Schneider, *Our Bloc: How We Win* (Verso, 2022), p. 31

92. Eunice Goss, "Pragmatic, Social, Democratic, Radical", in *The Starmer Symptom*, ed. Mark Perryman (Pluto, 2025), p. 251

93. Teddy Goldsmith, *The Stable Society* (Wadebridge Press, 1978)

94. UK Green History. Ecology Party Election Manifesto. 1975. https://green-history.uk/j3/library/doc-archive/file/162-ecology-party-manifesto-for-a-sustainable-society-1975

95. UK Green History. Ecology Party Manifesto for a Sustainable Society. 1979. https://green-history.uk/j3/library/doc-archive/file/22-dt0030-ecologyparty1979electionmanifesto

96. UK Green History. Ecology Party Manifesto. General Election. 1983. https://green-history.uk/j3/library/doc-archive/file/106-ecology-party-manifesto-1983-general-election

97. *The New Statesman*. Steve Reed's £7bn affordable housing fund. 7 November 2025. www.newstatesman.com/podcasts/politics-podcast/2025/11/steve-reeds-7bn-affordable-housing-fund

98. Abolish Landlords, text publicly accessible at: www.alexandersallons.com/abolishlandlords

99. Andrew Murray, *Is Socialism Possible in Britain? Reflections on the Corbyn Years* (Verso, 2022), p. 86

100. *The Guardian*. Clause IV: A brief history. 9 August 2015. www.theguardian.com/politics/2015/aug/09/clause-iv-of-labour-

party-constitution-what-is-all-the-fuss-about-reinstating-it
101. *The Guardian*. Owen Jones meets Caroline Lucas. 31 July 2015. www.youtube.com/watch?v=iFG3INb7VWU&t=102s
102. Jason W. Moore, *Capitalism in the Web of Life: Ecology and the Accumulation of Capital* (Verso, 2015)
103. Naomi Klein, *This Changes Everything: Capitalism vs. the Climate* (Simon & Schuster, 2014)
104. Chris Saltmarsh, *Burnt* (Pluto, 2021), p. 47; Saltmarsh, *Burnt*, p. 23
105. Another Green World. When Keir Starmer was Marxist. 4 April 2020. https://another-green-world.blogspot.com/2020/04/when-keir-starmer-was-marxist.html
106. Capitalism Nature Socialism. An Ecosocialist Manifesto. September 2001. www.cnsjournal.org/an-ecosocialist-manifesto/
107. Derek Wall, *The Rise of the Green Left* (Pluto, 2010), p. 134
108. Matthew T. Huber, *Climate Change as Class War: Building Socialism on a Warming Planet* (Verso, 2022), p. 6
109. Politics Home. Support for Labour has collapsed among teachers, union poll shows. 7 January 2026. www.politicshome.com/news/article/labour-support-among-neu-teachers-collapses-poll-finds
110. BBC News. Keir Starmer speech: Labour leader to quote Tony Blair in pitch for power. 27 September 2022. www.bbc.co.uk/news/uk-politics-63037696
111. *The Guardian*. Unite announces cut to Labour membership fees by £580,000. 11 March 2026. www.theguardian.com/uk-news/2026/mar/11/unite-announces-cut-to-labour-membership-fees-by-more-than-half-a-million-pounds
112. GMB London Region. Heathrow third runway will create

"thousands of good jobs". 29 January 2025. www.gmblondon.org.uk/news/heathrow-third-runway-will-create-thousands-of-good-jobs

113. Novara Media. Greens most popular party among voters under 65. 4 March 2026. https://novaramedia.com/2026/03/04/greens-most-popular-party-among-voters-under-65/

114. Green Party of England and Wales. Green Party Workers' Charter 2026. https://greenparty.org.uk/workerscharter/

115. Roger Scruton, *Green Philosophy: How to Think Seriously about the Planet* (Atlantic, 2012), p. 27

116. Jonathan Porritt and David Winner, *The Coming of the Greens* (William Collins, 1988), p. 19

117. Grace Blakeley, *Vulture Capitalism: How to Survive in an Age of Corporate Greed* (Bloomsbury, 2024)

118. The London Weekend Return Group, *In and Against the State: Discussion Notes for Socialists*, new edition (Pluto, 2021)

119. Geoff Mann and Joel Wainwright, *Climate Leviathan: A Political Theory of Our Planetary Future* (Verso, 2018)

120. Kent County Council. Kent County Council elections. www.kent.gov.uk/about-the-council/how-the-council-works/kent-county-council-elections

121. BBC News. "Nasty" councillor jailed for coercive behaviour. 20 February 2026. www.bbc.co.uk/news/articles/c627ngz1k1eo

122. Kent County Council. Kent County Council elections. www.kent.gov.uk/about-the-council/how-the-council-works/kent-county-council-elections

123. Kent County Council. Kent County Council elections. www.kent.gov.uk/about-the-council/how-the-council-works/kent-county-council-elections

124. UK Parliament. North Herefordshire. https://members.par-

liament.uk/constituency/4210/election/422
125. UK Parliament. Waveney Valley. https://members.parliament.uk/constituency/4384/election/422
126. Open Council Data UK. Party Totals Archive 2016–26. https://opencouncildata.co.uk/councillors2.php?y=0
127. BBC News. England local election results 2023. www.bbc.co.uk/news/election/2023/england/results
128. YouGov. Political trackers (9–10 Sept update). 2019. https://yougov.com/en-gb/articles/24985-political-trackers-9-10-sept
129. BBC News. Election 2019. www.bbc.co.uk/news/election/2019/results
130. BBC News. Lewisham Council Results. www.bbc.co.uk/news/election/2026/england/councils/E09000023
131. BBC News. Greens "on course for record-breaking elections". 9 April 2026. www.bbc.co.uk/news/articles/cj94ywnwy9ro
132. BBC News. Green Party's new MP calls for pause on pylons. 9 July 2024. www.bbc.co.uk/news/articles/cgrlx7z64n40
133. *Crowborough News* (2025) Angry Crowborough residents pack community meeting to discuss asylum seeker plans. 13 November 2025. https://crowborough.news/angry-crowborough-residents-pack-community-meeting-to-discuss-asylum-seeker-plans/
134. Friends of the Earth. Toxic air increasingly harming those least responsible. 5 November 2025. https://friendsoftheearth.uk/latest/toxic-air-increasingly-harming-those-least-responsible
135. Ezra Klein and Derek Thompson, *Abundance* (Avid Reader Press, 2025)
136. London Centric. Who's behind London's vigilante tube cleaners? 14 June 2025. www.londoncentric.media/p/looking-for-growth-bakerloo-line-graffiti-dominic-cummings

137. New Economics Foundation. Expanding UK airports won't deliver economic growth. 22 January 2025. https://neweconomics.org/2025/01/expanding-uk-airports-wont-deliver-economic-growth
138. *The Independent*. Reeves launches fresh war on bats and newts to speed up development. 18 August 2025. www.independent.co.uk/news/uk/politics/rachel-reeves-planning-infrastructure-bill-hs2-b2809277.html
139. Wildlife Trusts. Planning and development: Nature isn't the problem. May 2025. www.wildlifetrusts.org/sites/default/files/2025-05/Planning%20on%20bats%20and%20newts%20-%20FullReport.pdf
140. Jonathan Porritt and David Winner, *The Coming of the Greens* (William Collins, 1988), p. 17.
141. Guy Shrubsole, *Who Owns England?* (William Collins, 2019)
142. Rebecca Smith, *Rural: The Lives of the Working Class Countryside* (William Collins, 2023)
143. BBC News. Supreme Court backs wild camping on Dartmoor. 21 May 2025. www.bbc.co.uk/news/articles/cwywwq5zkqwo
144. Rural England. Poverty in Rural England. 2020. https://ruralengland.org/wp-content/uploads/2020/04/1.-Briefing-note-on-rural-poverty-Shucksmith.pdf
145. Department for Energy Security and Net Zero. Fuel Poverty Strategy for England. 26 January 2026. www.gov.uk/government/publications/fuel-poverty-strategy-for-england/fuel-poverty-strategy-for-england--2
146. HuffPost. I was one of the first Extinction Rebellion protestors to be arrested: Here's why I have no regrets. 22 April 2019. www.huffingtonpost.co.uk/entry/extinction-rebellion-arrests_uk_5cbcdd5de4b032e7ceb9bb92

147. BBC News. Green MP Caroline Lucas arrested at climate protest. 19 August 2013. www.bbc.co.uk/news/uk-england-23753750; *The Standard*. Extinction Rebellion protests: Green Party co-leader Jonathan Bartley and climate activist George Monbiot arrested on Whitehall. 16 October 2019. www.standard.co.uk/news/london/extinction-rebellion-protests-green-party-coleader-jonathan-bartley-and-climate-activist-george-monbiot-arrested-on-whitehall-a4263361.html

148. LBC. MEP tells LBC about her arrest after defending Extinction Rebellion's right to protest. 15 October 2019. www.lbc.co.uk/article/mep-tells-lbc-about-her-arrest-after-defending-xr-DWySwq_2/

149. BBC News. Greek compromise: How Syriza has had to change its plans. 24 February 2015. www.bbc.com/news/world-europe-31003070

150. Michael Chessum, *This Is Only the Beginning: The Making of a New Left – From Anti-Austerity to the Fall of Corbyn* (Bloomsbury, 2022)

151. *The New Statesman*. Starmer would "love" to "team up" with the right. 21 October 2025. www.youtube.com/watch?v=ci4sPbVncEc

152. Richard Seymour, *Corbyn: The Strange Rebirth of Radical Politics* (Verso, 2016), p. 205

153. Greens Organise (2026) Pledge to oppose austerity in local government. https://greensorganise.uk/pledge-oppose-austerity/

154. transform! europe. The Workers' Party of Belgium: Success in the municipal elections. 5 November 2024. https://transform-network.net/blog/analysis/the-workers-party-of-belgium-success-in-the-municipal-elections/

155. Instagram. @hannahtheplumbermcr. 30 September 2025. www.instagram.com/reel/DPONjmSihAg/?igsh=MTNsbmJ1dmR2dHd4YQ%3D%3D

156. Adam Greenfield, *Lifehouse: Taking Care of Ourselves in a World on Fire* (Verso, 2024), p. 21

157. Greenfield, *Lifehouse*, p. 168

158. Greenfield, *Lifehouse*, p. 193

159. *The Guardian*. Corbyn tells Labour councils to hold back on illegal budget-setting. 18 December 2015. www.theguardian.com/politics/2015/dec/18/corbyn-local-labour-councils-illegal-budget-setting-cuts

160. Abundance. Popular asset commissions: Building a Green democratic Haringey. 17 March 2026. www.in-abundance.org/latest/pacsharingey

161. Lisa Nandy, Caroline Lucas and Chris Bowes (eds), *The Alternative: Towards a New Progressive Politics* (Biteback, 2016)

162. Compass. The Green's new deal: Reaction to Zack Polanski's victory in the Green Party leadership election with Jonathan Bartley. 2 September 2025. www.compassonline.org.uk/podcast/upcoming/the-greens-new-deal-reaction-to-zack-polanskis-victory-in-the-green-party-leadership-election-with-jonathan-bartley/

163. *The Guardian*. Andy Burnham to back electoral reform if he becomes prime minister. 21 May 2026. www.theguardian.com/politics/2026/may/21/andy-burnham-back-electoral-reform-if-prime-minister

164. Anton Jager, *Hyperpolitics* (Verso, 2026)

165. Keir Milburn, *Generation Left* (Polity, 2019), pp. 100–1

166. Seymour, *Corbyn*, p. 189

167. House of Commons Library. Membership of political parties

in Great Britain. 30 August 2022. https://researchbriefings.files.parliament.uk/documents/SN05125/SN05125.pdf

168. Jager, *Hyperpolitics*, p. 91

169. X. @timesradio. 23 October 2025. https://x.com/TimesRadio/status/1981345853424963617

170. YouGov. How do Britons see the main political parties, autumn 2025? 9 October 2025. https://yougov.com/en-gb/articles/53137-how-do-britons-see-the-main-political-parties-autumn-2025

171. YouGov. How do Green Party members feel about the party, its leaders, and seeking power? 3 October 2025. https://yougov.com/en-gb/articles/53108-how-do-green-party-members-feel-about-the-party-its-leaders-and-seeking-power

172. Jonathan Porritt and David Winner, *The Coming of the Greens* (William Collins, 1988), p. 9

173. Oxfam. Billionaires emit more carbon pollution in under three hours than the average Brit does in a lifetime. 28 October 2024. www.oxfam.org.uk/media/press-releases/billionaires-emit-more-carbon-pollution-in-under-three-hours-than-the-average-brit-does-in-a-lifetime/

174. Oxfam International. Richest 1% emit as much planet-heating pollution as two-thirds of humanity. 20 November 2023. www.oxfam.org/en/press-releases/richest-1-emit-much-planet-heating-pollution-two-thirds-humanity

175. BBC News. A few frequent flyers "dominate air travel". 31 March 2021. www.bbc.co.uk/news/science-environment-56582094

176. Possible. Jetting away with it. 19 July 2023. www.wearepossible.org/latest-news/jetting-away-with-it

177. *The Guardian*. Earth's ozone layer on course to be healed

within decades, UN report finds. 9 January 2023. www.theguardian.com/environment/2023/jan/09/ozone-layer-healed-within-decades-un-report

178. Naomi Klein, *This Changes Everything: Capitalism vs. the Climate* (Simon & Schuster, 2014), p. 64

179. Adrienne Buller, *The Value of a Whale: On the Illusions of Green Capitalism* (Manchester University Press, 2022)

180. *The Guardian*. Carbon offsets fail to cut global heating due to "intractable" systemic problems, study says. 6 October 2025. www.theguardian.com/environment/2025/oct/06/carbon-offsets-fail-cut-global-heating-intractable-systemic-problems-study

181. BBC News. Trump revokes landmark ruling that greenhouse gases endanger public health. 12 February 2026. www.bbc.co.uk/news/articles/cnozdd7yl4vo; *The New York Times*. Trump eases restrictions on climate "super pollutants". 21 May 2026. www.nytimes.com/2026/05/21/climate/trump-super-pollutants-hfc-epa-climate-change.html

182. E. F. Schumacher, *Small Is Beautiful: Economics as If People Mattered* (Blond and Briggs, 1973)

183. Kate Soper, *Post-Growth Living: For an Alternative Hedonism* (Verso, 2023)

184. Kate Raworth, *Donut Economics: Seven Ways to Think Like a 21st-Century Economist* (Random House, 2017)

185. Matthew T. Huber, *Climate Change as Class War: Building Socialism on a Warming Planet* (Verso, 2022), p. 51

186. More In Common. Sceptical scrollers. www.moreincommon.org.uk/seven-segments/sceptical-scrollers/

187. *The Guardian*. Far right trying to infiltrate UK's low-traffic protests, campaigners warn. 24 February 2023. www.theguardian.

com/world/2023/feb/24/far-right-trying-to-infiltrate-low-traffic-protests-campaigners-warn

188. BBC News. 15 minute cities: How they got caught in conspiracy theories. 3 October 2023. www.bbc.co.uk/news/uk-politics-66990302; BBC News. Rishi Sunak: Cars, boilers and net zero – key takeaways from PM's speech. 20 September 2023. www.bbc.co.uk/news/uk-66871073; *The Guardian*. Kemi Badenoch vows to repeal Climate Change Act. 2 October 2025. www.theguardian.com/environment/2025/oct/02/kemi-badenoch-vows-to-repeal-climate-change-act

189. *The Guardian*. Rightwing narrative fuelling false belief UK public oppose net zero, study finds. 20 March 2026. www.theguardian.com/environment/2026/mar/20/uk-public-support-net-zero-rightwing-media-rories-reform-analysis

190. Climate Change Committee. Cost of Net Zero by 2050 less than a single fossil fuel price shock – CCC. 11 March 2026. www.theccc.org.uk/2026/03/11/cost-of-net-zero-by-2050-less-than-a-single-fossil-fuel-price-shock-ccc/

191. Brett Christophers, *The Price Is Wrong: Why Capitalism Won't Save the Planet* (Verso, 2024)

192. YouGov. Most Britons think water and energy companies should be nationalised. 27 May 2026. https://yougov.com/en-gb/articles/54846-most-britons-think-water-and-energy-companies-should-be-nationalised

193. James Meadway, "There Is Always an Alternative", in *The Starmer Symptom*, ed. Mark Perryman (Pluto, 2025), p. 175

194. *The Telegraph*. Soaring food prices have brought down governments for centuries. Labour could be next. 18 January 2026. www.telegraph.co.uk/money/consumer-affairs/soaring-food-prices-

brought-down-governments-labour-next/
195. *The Guardian*. Squeals of horror over price caps: But how are we going to fix our broken food system? 24 May 2026. www.theguardian.com/business/2026/may/24/horror-price-caps-fix-broken-food-system-analysis
196. *The Financial Times*. UK Treasury pushes supermarkets to cap food prices. 19 May 2026. www.ft.com/content/85736371-40bc-4ec1-a502-4f557d3a68b0?syn-25a6b1a6=1
197. *The Financial Times*. Rachel Reeves drops push for food price cap after retail backlash. 20 May 2026. www.ft.com/content/636b9473-0488-4d72-98ae-55ff008d7221?syn-25a6b1a6=1
198. *The New York Times*. Mamdani's first city-owned grocery store is planned for the south Bronx. 18 May 2026. www.nytimes.com/2026/05/18/nyregion/mamdani-grocery-store-bronx-hunts-point.html
199. Naked Politics. Zack Polanski is cooking: Could this be the start of a new politics? 10 September 2025. www.nakedpolitics.co.uk/zack-polanski-is-cooking-could-this-be-the-start-of-a-new-politics/
200. BBC News. Morrisons planning to close 100 stores in next few months. 22 May 2026. www.bbc.co.uk/news/articles/c3623n-y298x0
201. X. @meadwaj. 22 May 2026. https://x.com/meadwaj/status/2057789543563042919
202. Campaign to Protect Rural England. Council farms: What are they, and why are they so special? 14 May 2021. www.cpre.org.uk/explainer/county-farms-explainer/
203. Fairness Foundation. Wealth gap risk register. 27 October 2025. https://fairnessfoundation.com/risks-2025

204. X. @zackpolanski. 9 March 2026. https://x.com/ZackPolanski/status/2030992446805389482

205. *The Standard*. "I was facing 10 years in jail", says Green candidate in London caught smuggling 10,000 ecstasy tablets into LA. 17 April 2026. www.standard.co.uk/news/politics/green-candidate-london-prison-smuggle-drugs-ecstasy-los-angeles-america-b1279111.html

206. *The Telegraph*. Greens deputy leader shared conspiracy theory over Golders Green attack. 6 May 2026. www.telegraph.co.uk/politics/2026/05/05/green-party-anti-semitism-local-election-sabine-mairey/

207. *The Independent*. Pro-Palestine protest organisers slam Met Police chief over "defamatory" synagogue march route claims. 4 May 2026. www.independent.co.uk/news/uk/home-news/palestine-coalition-met-police-mark-rowley-synagogues-b2970176.html

208. *The Guardian*. Badenoch defends seeking a ban on pro-Palestine marches but not Tommy Robinson ones – as it happened. 5 May 2026. www.theguardian.com/politics/live/2026/may/05/keir-starmer-uk-antisemitism-summit-golders-green-terror-latest-news-updates

209. *The Guardian*. Anti-Islam influencer Valentina Gomez blocked from entering UK for far-right rally. 20 April 2026. www.theguardian.com/world/2026/apr/20/anti-islam-influencer-valentina-gomez-blocked-uk-far-right-rally

210. Sky News. Polanski questioned over sharing social media criticism of Golders Green policing. 3 May 2026. https://news.sky.com/video/polanski-questioned-over-sharing-social-media-criticism-of-golders-green-policing-13539629

211. *The Independent*. Polanski wrongly claims Golders Green

terror suspect was handcuffed in video that sparked row with Met Police. 6 May 2026. www.independent.co.uk/news/uk/politics/polanski-police-golders-green-video-met-police-b2971310.html

212. *The Independent*. "No country has right to exist", says Polanski in response to Israel question. 7 May 2026. www.independent.co.uk/bulletin/news/zack-polanski-peston-itv-israel-b2972128.html

213. *The Independent*. Polanski's popularity plummets following row with police chief over his Golders Green response. 6 May 2026. www.independent.co.uk/news/uk/politics/zack-polanski-green-party-local-elections-golders-green-b2971209.html

214. X. @chris_annous. 7 May 2026. https://x.com/chris_annous/status/2052162224232501395

215. BBC News. England Local election results 2026. www.bbc.co.uk/news/election/2026/england/results

216. ITV News. "Historic breakthrough" for Green Party in Wales as first two MSs elected to the Senedd. 8 May 2026. www.itv.com/news/wales/2026-05-08/first-ever-green-ms-as-party-leader-anthony-slaughter-wins-seat

217. Electoral Reform Society. How would each party have done if May's elections were across all of Britain? 18 May 2026. https://electoral-reform.org.uk/how-would-each-party-have-done-if-mays-elections-were-across-all-of-britain/

218. *The New Statesman*. Are the Greens taking Reform votes? 3 March 2026. www.newstatesman.com/politics/uk-politics/2026/03/are-the-greens-taking-reform-votes

219. Common Wealth. Popular radicalism in post-industrial England. 2026. www.common-wealth.org/interactive/popular-radicalism-in-post-industrial-england

220. BBC News. Starmer: If you don't like Labour changes leave.

15 February 2023. www.bbc.co.uk/news/av/uk-politics-64649299

221. X. @lukeakehurst. 11 May 2026. https://x.com/lukeakehurst/status/2053767329108902226

222. BBC News. Birmingham local election results 2026. www.bbc.co.uk/news/election/2026/england/councils/E08000025

223. Rebecca Solnit, *Hope in the Dark* (Canongate, 2010), p. 29